SLIPPING AWAY

Complete Parent's Guide To Recognizing Teen Drug Experimentation and Abuse

Insider Secrets The Experts Don't Tell You

JENNIFER KOBUKI

Slipping Away

Complete Parent's Guide To Recognizing Teen Drug Experimentation and Abuse

www.SlippingAwayBook.com

www.JenniferKobuki.com

Disclaimer: This book is designed solely for educational and informational purposes. The author and publisher are not offering any professional advice of any kind. The content of this book is the sole expression and opinion of the author. In the case of a need for such expertise, consult with the appropriate professional. While best efforts have been used in preparing this book, the author and publisher make no representations or warranties of any kind and assume no liabilities of any kind with respect to the accuracy or completeness of the contents. Neither the author nor the publisher shall be held liable or responsible to any person or entity with respect to any damages caused, directly or indirectly, by the information contained herein.

ISBN: 978-0-578-14399-6

Library of Congress Control Number: 2014912211

Printed in the United States of America.

DEDICATION

This book is dedicated to my mother, Sue, who is always supporting me and believing in me even when I stopped believing in myself. To the parents of teenagers, never lose hope for a brighter tomorrow.

CONTENTS

ACKNOWLEDGMENTS

A big thank you to all of the ladies at OCJ for all of your valuable insight and feedback. Your contribution was vital to the research that was put into this guide. Thank you to the justice system for my opportunity to stay in your county jail. If it were not for the 8 months I was incarcerated I would not have realized my calling in life.

My dear friend, Billy Chamberlin, your life experiences through addiction and recovery make you a true role model for anyone battling addiction. Through your sobriety and the sobriety of others, together we will change lives.

Thank you Michael Stevenson of Transform Destiny for all of your knowledge and guidance in bringing this guide together. It would not have been possible without you.

I owe the biggest thank you of all to my mother, Sue. Through my ups and downs, you have always stood by my side. You are my best friend, role model, and a true inspiration. You always saw the good in me even when I could not see it in myself. Thank you for never losing faith and hope when everyone told you it was gone. I am blessed every day to have a mother like you. I love you. You inspired me to take my life experiences and help other parents who may be struggling with the same issues.

YOU FAILED TO UNDERSTAND

You saw the grades fall
And the set of new friends.
You thought nothing at all
Of the new styles and trends.
Arguments each night.
And try as you might
You failed to understand, or comprehend.

You got notes from the school.
You heard of pressure from peers.
You felt such a fool
So you didn't interfere.
The actions were rash.
You were missing some cash.
You failed to understand, or comprehend.

It pulled you apart.
Then the missing car keys
Was a punch to the heart
And you fell to your knees.
Death sat in the eyes.
With life paralyzed,
You failed to understand, or comprehend.

By Dr. Jan Musgrove

INTRODUCTION

1.4 million American teens have a drug abuse problem.

"Drugfree.org"

Have you noticed a change in your teens attitude and/or behavior? Do they seem more withdrawn than usual? Have you noticed a sudden change in their appearance or behavior? Do you find yourself questioning the friends your teen is hanging out with?

If you answered yes to any of those questions then this guide is for you. The fact that you are picking up this guide means that you have questions. The answers to these questions are within your teen if you only knew where to look. Drug abuse is a growing problem amongst teens and I believe that it is largely because the parents simply are not recognizing the warning signs.

Whether it be bits and pieces of drug materials lying around their room, slang terms used among their friends, physical or behavior changes, there are some things that every parent needs to be aware of. Your teen probably won't just leave their bag of drugs visibly on their dresser. There are other items that your teen will leave lying around their room or in their trash can because they do not think that their parents will know what it is used for. This guide is going to show you what those items may be. Usually by the time parents are aware of a drug problem their teen has either been arrested, dropped out of school, is failing classes, has overdosed, or have a major addiction.

When I was a teen my mom used to tell me, "You are who you hang out with," and she couldn't have been more right. You don't need to be a nosy parent but you do need to pay attention to who your teen is choosing to surround themselves with. If your teen is missing school to hang out with their friends, suddenly getting lower grades than usual, or changing their appearance or behavior then it's time to start asking questions. The teens that are experimenting with drugs are not always the obvious trouble makers or outsiders. Drugs are very common among the popular crowds at school, the party goers, and all other groups of teens. My point is, drugs are a growing problem in our country and its starting when they are just a teen. And no teen is the exception. When a teen experiments with drugs they invite some very dishonest, irresponsible, drug abusing friends into their life. They start to hang around with the wrong type of people, neglect responsibilities, commit crimes without thinking about it, steal from family members to buy drugs, drop out of school and sports, lose their job, and just really damage their lives. You can never ruin your life but drugs will certainly damage it.

According to the University of Michigan's Monitoring the Future Survey, more than 10 percent of high school seniors in the United States abused narcotics (other than heroin) at least once in their lifetime. Nearly 17 percent abused amphetamines, 10 percent abused barbiturates, and 11 percent abused tranquilizers at least once. Those numbers are alarming! Personally, I think the amount of teens experimenting with drugs is actually much larger than that.

When was the last time you sat down at your dinner table as a family? When was the last time you went out with your teen without your cell phones? Is there arguing in your house? Does your job keep you away from home? Most parents don't think that typical family life has an effect on their teen but you couldn't be more wrong. Family time isn't spent together like it used to be. There are more divorced households now than ever before, family dinners are rare, there is an absent parent from the household, parent's argue in front of the children, and families spend all their time on their cell phones when they go out together.

If any of these just described your family then you need to listen up. Your teen is at a critical stage in their life cycle. They need family support, love, communication and family involvement in their life. If they don't receive that at home then they are going to look to their friends to fill that void. When teens look to their friends to fill a void that they aren't getting at home then that is typically when drugs are introduced. Because they lean on the wrong type of friends. Drugs help take their mind off of problems they are having at home, school, or in their love life. You need to be involved in your teens life and I can't stress that enough. Spend time with your teen and most importantly, listen to them.

As a parent you need to understand that there are just things that a teen is not going to discuss with you and drugs is one of them. We were all a teen at one time, and I think it's really important to remember that. You remember hiding things from your parents so why would your teen be any different? Teens are in the independent and socialization stage of their life and that's a reality. We as parents need to be able to recognize certain behavior changes in our teen so that we can tell the difference between typical teenage behavior and drug abuse behavior. This reference guide is going to show you how to recognize drug abuse behavior. When I was a teen I encountered several police officers, even walked into a police station, totally high on drugs and the police officers never even noticed. No disrespect to police officers, but the fact is, unless you have used drugs yourself or been around drug abusers then you just don't know what to look for aside from the obvious signs.

My mother was my inspiration for writing this guide. I will never forget when she called me to discuss a conversation that she overheard my brother and his friends talking about when he was a teenager. She told me that she overheard them talking about being "blown on yay" and wanted to know if I knew what they were talking about. Right away I knew that they were using cocaine based on the language that they used. Then I started thinking, how many other parents don't know that their teen is abusing drugs because they don't recognize the language their teen is using among their friends, certain paraphernalia laying around their teens room, or physical and behavior changes that drug abuse is causing.

I can tell if someone is using drugs within the first five minutes of meeting them, and most of the time I can tell exactly what drug they are using. My goal is to have parents just like you be able to do the same thing. It's time to take the blindfolds off. I want you to know the warning signs when you see them.

Through my own addictions and the addictions of others, I will expose the secrets your teen does not want you to know. This reference guide is written solely from the interviews of former and current drug abusers and my personal drug abuse experience. No medical professionals, law enforcement, or legal guides were used. Instead I went straight to the real experts, the drug users themselves.

"What you choose to do one night can impact the rest of your life"

– Jennifer Kobuki

ALCOHOL

al ◦ co ◦ hol

intoxicating colorless liquid for drinks

"Of all vices, drinking is the most incompatible with greatness"

– Sir Walter Scott

ALCOHOL

Nearly 10 million youths, ages 12 to 20, in this country report they have consumed alcohol in the past 30 days. The rate of current alcohol consumption increases with age from 2% at age 12, 21% at age 16, and 55% at age 20.

"2011 National Survey on Drug Use and Health"

Alcohol is the most common substance abused by teens and I believe it's because it is so easily accessible. Think about it, I'm sure you have alcohol in your house. And where is it located? I'm pretty sure it's placed somewhere in your house where your teen has access to it.

Let's not be naïve. Your teen is probably going to experiment with alcohol at some point in their teen years. Did you or someone you know? When your teen gets together with their friends and they go to a party, there is probably going to be alcohol there. Alcohol was at all the parties I attended throughout my high school years. And every group of friends has a friend who can get them alcohol. It doesn't mean that you should never let your teen go out with their friends, but you do need to be aware of the warning signs. Whether it be at home, at a friend's house, or at a party. The reality is, once your child enters junior high or high school they are exposed to alcohol on a regular basis.

It's important to pay attention to your teens slang when talking to their friends, things your teen may leave lying around their room or in their trash can, physical and behavior changes so you can properly determine if they are using alcohol. By simply recognizing these things you can make a conscious decision whether you need to look a little further.

 **Slang Terms used to describe Alcohol:**

- Booze
- Drinks
- Cold one
- Juice
- Everclear
- Lik
- Brew
- Hard A
- Proof
- Jag
- Drank
- Brewsky
- Hard stuff
- Vino

Slang Terms used to describe how they feel:

- Drunk
- Buzzed
- Hammered
- Burnt
- Gone
- Chill-axin
- Wasted
- Loaded
- Faded
- Tipsy
- Wrecked
- Smashed
- Shit faced
- Trashed
- Plastered
- Sloshed

Paraphernalia to look for:

Shot glasses

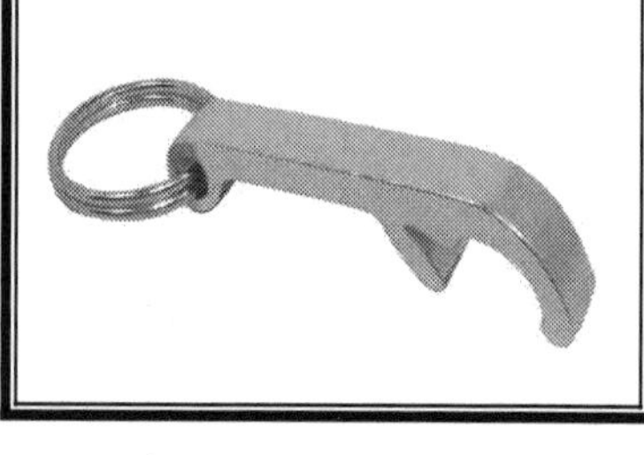

Bottle opener on key chain

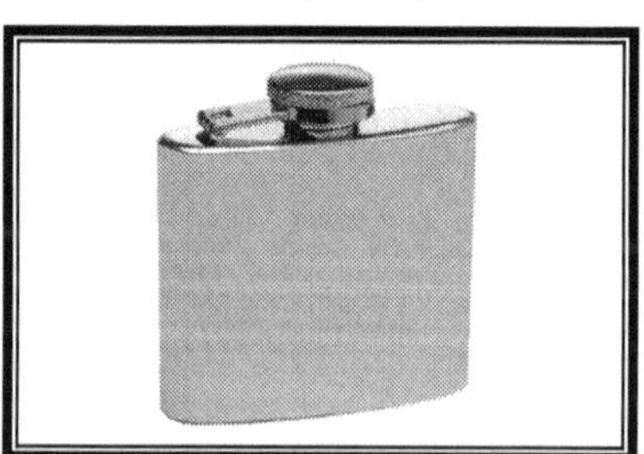

Flask

Party beer keg

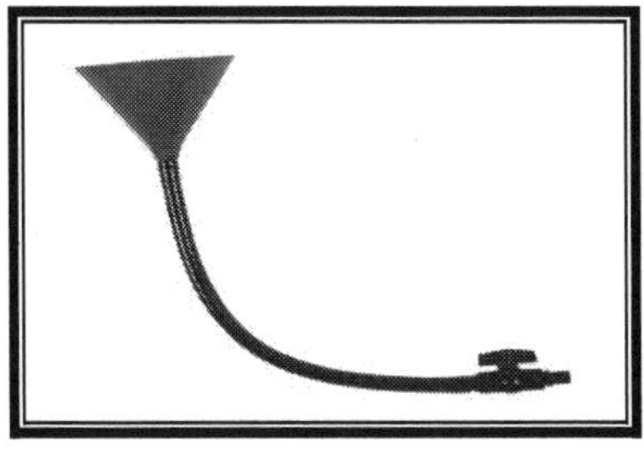

Beer bong – funnel with a clear hose

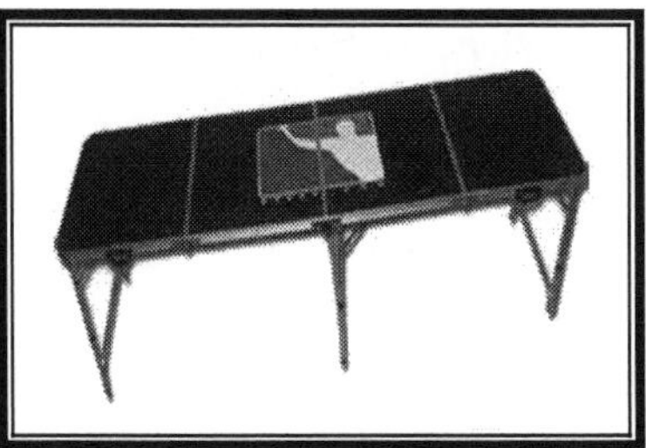

Beer pong table

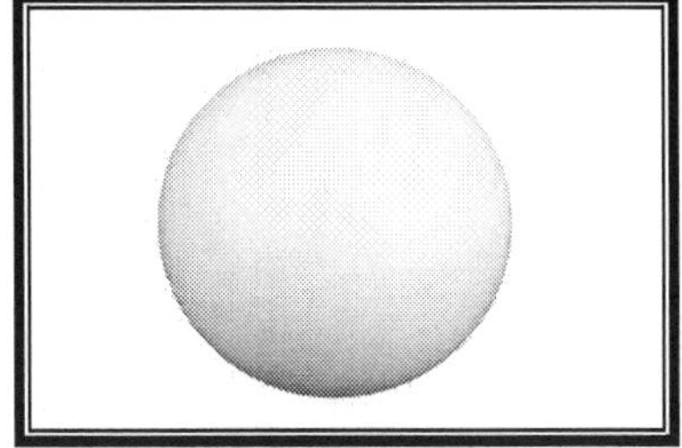

Ping pong balls

Plastic cups – typically red

Neon sign

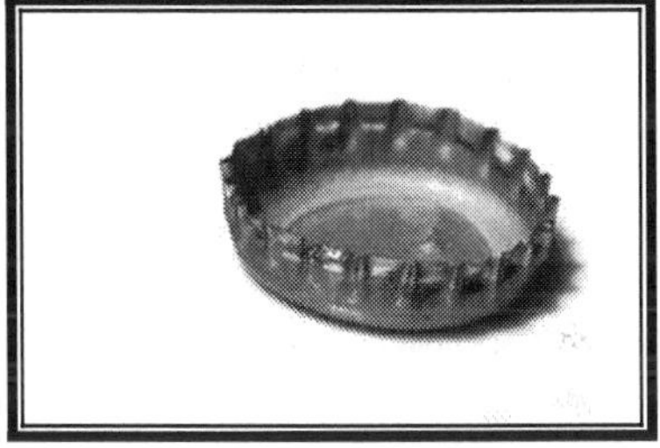

Bottle caps

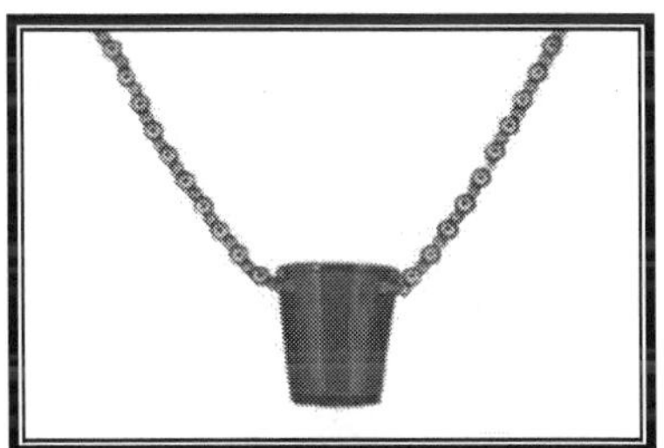

Shot glass necklaces

Physical changes:

When it comes to your teens physical appearance there are a few obvious signs to look out for. Slurred speech and staggered walking are the most obvious signs of alcohol abuse. Your teen may need assistance walking, standing upright, or even just keeping their head up. When I would go to parties, young girls would be so drunk they would lay all over the floor and just look very messy. Their makeup would be smudged and their hair a mess.

Since not everyone can handle too much alcohol it may also cause your teen to get sick, causing them to experience extreme vomiting and even blacking out. Your teen will have glassy and blood shot eyes while appearing to be barely keeping their eyes open. Not to mention their breath will smell like alcohol. No matter how much they try to conceal the smell it just doesn't work.

Weight gain is a good sign of long term alcohol abuse. When a teen drinks a lot they get hungry and over a period of time they gain excessive weight in their face and waist line. I can't express enough that all of these physical changes are just something that your teen will not be able to hide from you. You just need to pay attention.

Behavior changes:

The biggest behavior change when a teen has been consuming alcohol is impaired judgment. If your teen decides to drive home after they have had too much to drink, they can either be arrested for a DUI or even worse... injure or kill themselves or someone else. I have a friend that lost his arm and a few fingers because he got in the car with a drunk driver. I had another friend who drove through a park when he was drunk. My brother and his friend had to jump out of his car because they were in fear of their lives. You see, when you are a teen you determine the driver based on who has drank the least that night. That doesn't mean that they haven't drank any alcohol it just means that they haven't drank as much. Alcohol seems to take all the common sense out of teens and they will do things that they typically wouldn't do If they were not intoxicated.

I always describe intoxicated teens in 2 categories; happy or angry drunks. Happy drunks appear to be overly happy, loveable, giggly, chatty, and emotional. They love everyone and are very affectionate. Angry drunks, on the other hand, have severe mood swings causing them to get mad or confrontational easily. They will literally go from happy to mad at the drop of a hat. I have a few friends that when they get drunk they are looking for a fight. I don't think I have ever been to a party where there hasn't been a confrontation simply because they are intoxicated.

Alcohol abuse can cause your teen to neglect their responsibilities. They may start ditching school, stop doing their chores, excessive sleeping, frequent partying, and even stealing. When I was a teen my friends used to steal alcohol all the time from supermarkets and liquor stores. They called it a "beer run." That is when you pull up to a gas station, run inside and grab a few cases of beer, and run back out. It used to happen all the time. All of these behavior changes can be perceived as regular teenage behavior, however when these behavior changes are combined you need to realize that something more serious may be going on.

Let's not kid ourselves, we have all had a drink in our lifetime and we have all seen someone drunk before. It's very hard to hide too much alcohol consumption. When a teen has had too much to drink the signs are clearly there, you just need to know where to look. Your teen will do whatever they can to mask the smell of alcohol on their breath. You need to be smarter than your teen.

I would consider alcohol to be the true gateway to drugs. It really became reality to me not too long ago when I attended a New Year's eve party. This party had a lot of 17-18 year olds and I was amazed at how many of them were snorting cocaine, taking prescription drugs, and smoking marijuana all because they were drunk and other friends were doing it. When teens drink too much alcohol they are even more willing to experiment with drugs because they are "in the moment" and their friends are doing them.

You need to look beyond the obvious signs and stay in tune with your teen. Who they choose to surround themselves with, what you notice lying around their room no matter how small it may appear, along with your teens physical and/or behavior changes will all play a key role in knowing if your teen is hiding something from you. Don't be paranoid, just be aware!

MARIJUANA

mar ◦ i ◦ jua ◦ na

the dried leaves and flowers of the hemp plant that contain THC and is smoked as a drug

"I now have absolute proof that smoking even one marijuana cigarette is equal in brain damage to being on Bikini Island during a H-bomb blast"

– Ronald Reagan

MARIJUANA

Heavy marijuana use among teenagers is up 80 percent, with one in 10 teens reporting that they use the drug at least 20 times a month.

"The Partnership at Drugfree.org"

Marijuana is most commonly referred to as the gateway drug because it is typically the first drug that a teen will experiment with. Marijuana is one of the most frequently used drugs among teens and I believe that's because it's so easy to obtain. When I went to high school, there was marijuana at school and parties, it just seemed to be the "in thing" that all teens were doing. Marijuana has become more common amongst high school students than smoking cigarettes. According to the Partnership at Drugfree.org, "Heavy marijuana use among teenagers is up 80 percent, with one in ten teens reporting that they use the drug at least 20 times a month."

Although marijuana is probably the least dangerous drug out there, it can still have its negative effects on teens. Heavy marijuana use can cause teens to neglect their responsibilities, sleep excessively, fail classes or even drop out of school. In a nutshell, marijuana makes a teen very lazy and unmotivated. They don't want to do anything that requires too much effort or movement because that will "bring the high down."

It's important to pay attention to your teens slang when talking to their friends, things your teen may leave lying around their room or in their trash can, physical and behavior changes so you can properly determine if they are using marijuana. By simply recognizing these things you can make a conscious decision whether you need to look a little further.

Slang Terms used to describe Marijuana:

- Weed
- Trees
- Greens
- Ganja
- Mary Jane
- Reefer
- Hash
- Pot
- Herb
- 420
- Fire
- Bomb
- Dank
- Hydro
- Bud
- Chronic
- Cannabis
- Mary J
- Goodies
- Kush
- Stress

Slang Terms used to describe how they feel:

- Faded
- Stoned
- Blunted
- Blitzed
- Wrecked
- Baked
- Loaded
- Blazed
- Lit
- Smoked out
- High
- Blown
- Gone
- Toked

Paraphernalia to look for:

Rolling papers

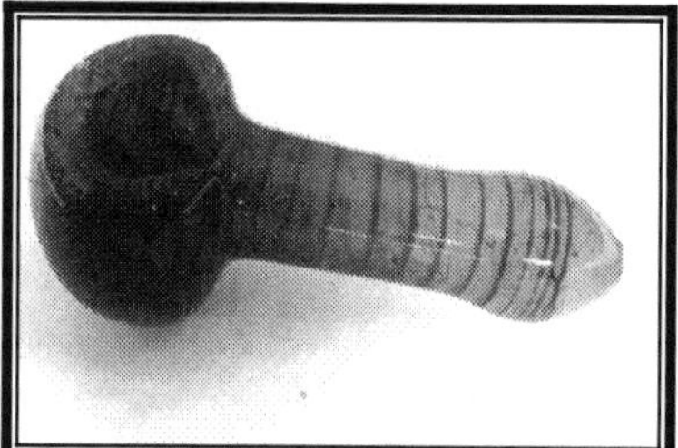

Glass pipe

Glass bong

Eye drops

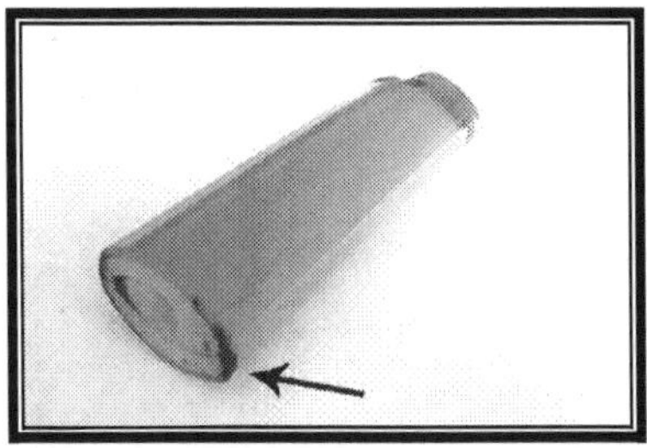

Lighters with burn marks on the bottom

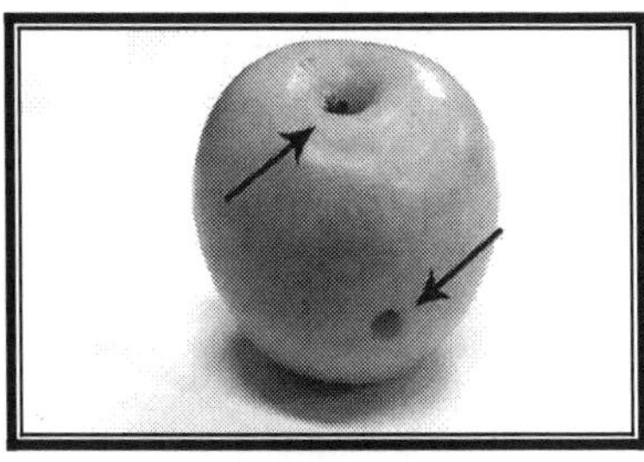

Apple with hole on top and the side

Cigar tobacco in trash can

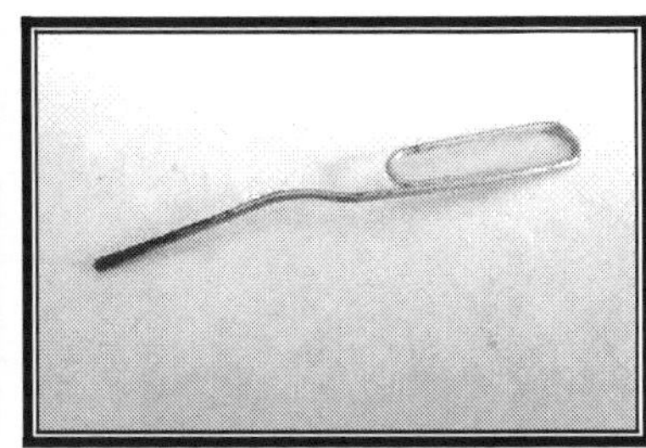

Straightened paper clip

Plastic baggies

Grinder

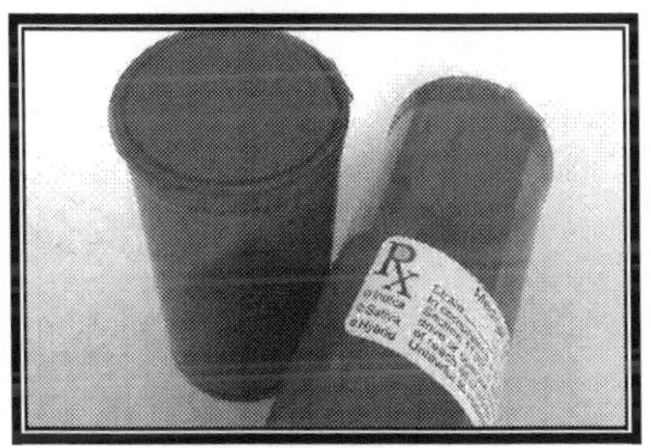

Prescription bottle

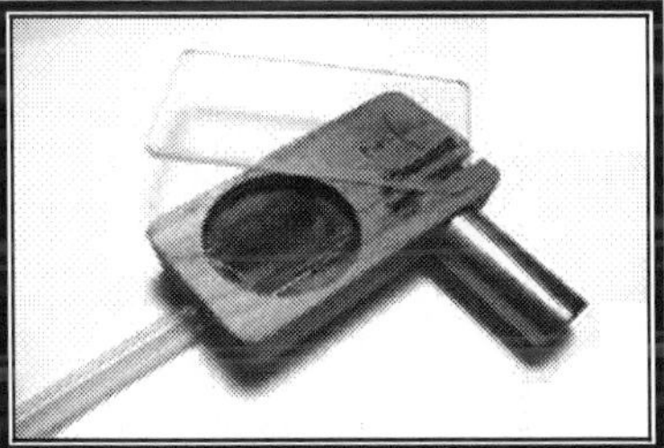

Vaporizer

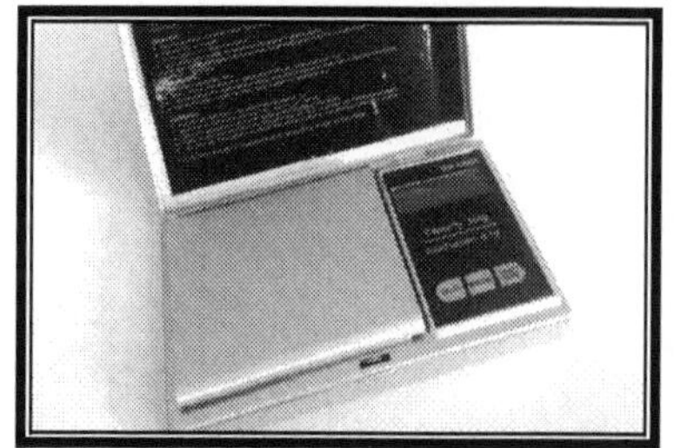

Handheld scale

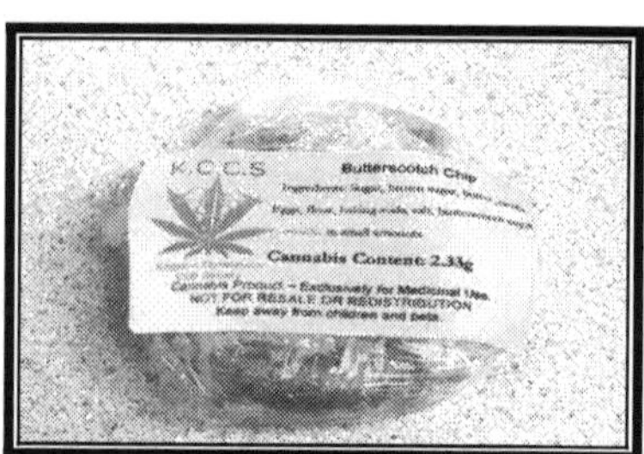

Desserts or candy in plastic wrap or bag with label on it

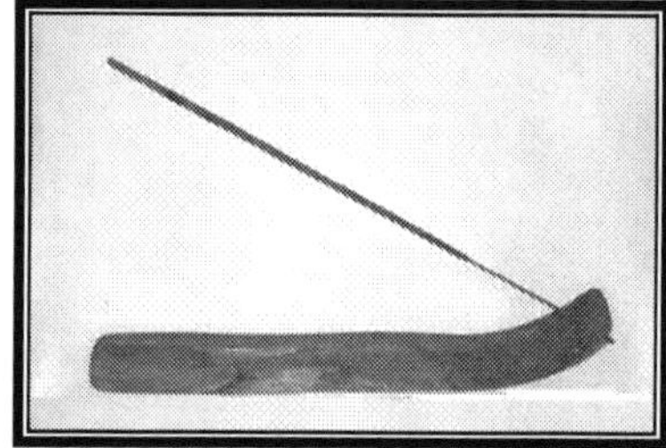

Incense

Deodorizer

Gas mask

Hookah

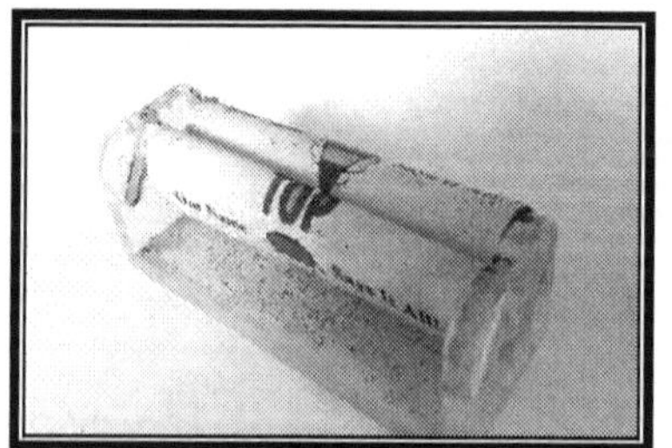

Tobacco / Join paper roller

Roaches in ashtray or trash can

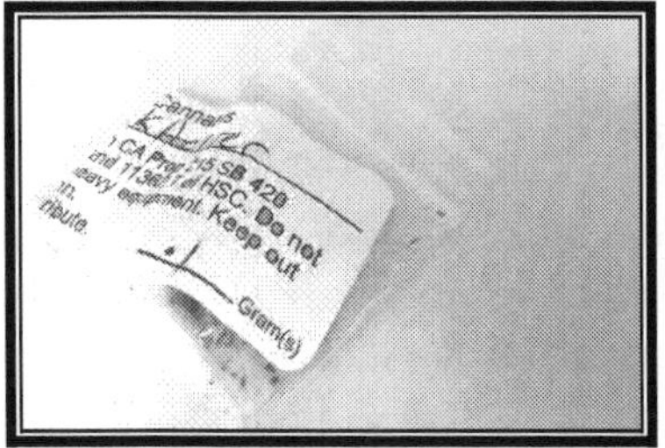

Small plastic baggie with sticker

Keif / Brown powder found in small plastic container

"Stash can" – can with a hidden compartment (it will look out of place like a coffee can or aerosol can in their room)

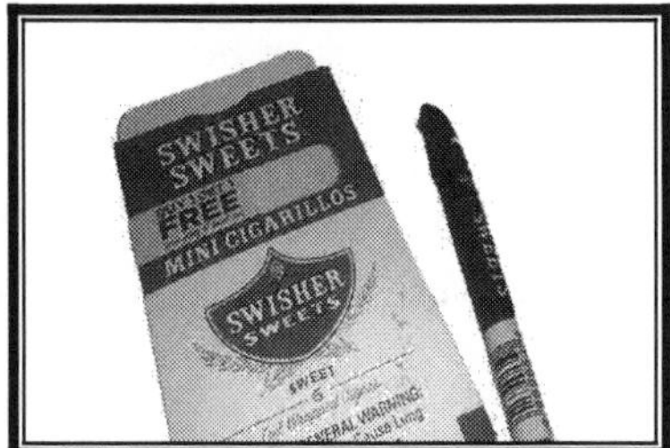

Cigars "Cigarillos"

⚠ **Physical changes:**

When it comes to your teens physical appearance, there are a few obvious signs to look out for. Blood shot and tired eyes are the strong indicator that your teen may be using marijuana. If your teen is smoking marijuana their eyes will be glossy, red, and very tired looking. Teens often try to hide their blood shot eyes by using eye drops so you need to look at other physical changes as well.

A increased appetite is referred to by most teens as having the munchies. Every marijuana user I have ever known got the munchies after smoking marijuana, it didn't matter what time of day it was. Along with an increased appetite will come weight gain and that's because they tend to have a craving for the sweet stuff and do a lot of laying or sitting around.

You may also notice that your teen has a "lazy" walk to them. Since smoking marijuana makes them very tired and relaxed they will walk around with a slouched look to them. They will also walk at a slower pace than they may naturally move.

⚠ **Behavior changes:**

The most common behavior change in a teen who smokes marijuana is their sleep patterns. Your teen will sleep excessively and at random times of the day. Since marijuana makes a person overly relaxed and they tend to just lay around, they may doze off shortly after they have smoked which then causes them to neglect their responsibilities. They may miss school, not do their homework, or fail to do chores because they would rather sleep.

You may also find that your teen is experiencing short term memory loss. You may ask your teen a question and it will take a minute for them to respond. They may even be in the middle of a conversation and forget what they were talking about. It happens all the time. When a teen has been using marijuana they may not even remember what they did an hour ago or can't remember where they put something. In a sense, it makes your teen temporarily dumb.

Other behavior changes are obvious mood swings, excessive giggling, and a sudden change in their friends. All of these behavior changes can be perceived as regular teenage behavior, however when these behavior changes are combined then you need to realize that something more serious may be going on.

Simply put, if you refuse to believe that your teen is using marijuana because you "raised them better than that" you may be sadly mistaken. I believe that most teens use marijuana simply because they do not perceive it to be a dangerous drug or even a drug at all. I have heard time and time again from frequent marijuana users that marijuana is not a drug, it is a herb because it grows from the ground rather than being a chemical. And my response is that it is a drug because it gives them an altered state of mind. My point is, if your teen doesn't perceive marijuana as a drug then they are more likely to use it.

I believe in being honest so it is my opinion that marijuana doesn't cause harmful effects to a person, however it does create an addictive personality which may later lead to your teen wanting to try another, more harmful drug.

You need to look beyond the obvious signs and stay in tune with your teen. Who they choose to surround themselves with, what you notice lying around their room no matter how small it may appear, along with your teens physical and/or behavior changes will all play a key role in knowing if your teen is hiding something from you. Don't be paranoid, just be aware!

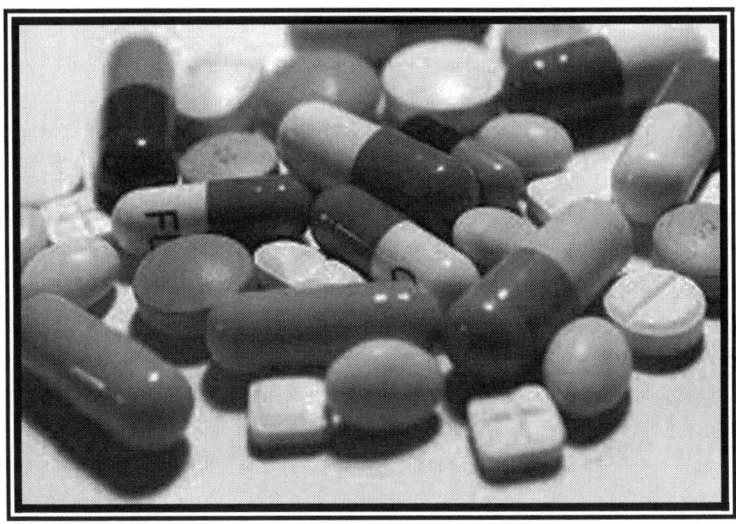

PRESCRIPTION DRUGS

pre ◦ scrip ◦ tion drug

drug available only by prescription: a drug that can be dispensed only with showing of a legally valid prescription

"Drugs have taught an entire generation of American kids the metric system"

– P.J. O'Rourke

PRESCRIPTION DRUGS

In 2009, a study found that one in five teenagers (20 percent) have taken prescription drugs without a doctor's prescription.

"CDC"

A new report shows that more people die from prescription drug overdoses than heroin and cocaine combined. Why are teens using prescription drugs? Because they think they are safer than street drugs and they may even be able to study more effectively. Not to mention, prescription drugs are easy for your teen to obtain. After all, these are the drugs that mom, dad, or their siblings are using right? These are the drugs that parents are leaving on counter tops, in medicine cabinets, and just lying around the house. Every teen knows someone at school who has medication and they have no problem passing it out to other students.

The prescription drugs most commonly abused by teens are Oxycodone (OxyContin, Percodan, Percocet), Hydrocodone (Vicodin, Norco, Lortab, Lorcet), Codeine, Xanax, Valium, Adderall, Demerol, and Ritalin. If you have prescriptions to any of those medications then I would suggest that you do not leave them out in the open. These medications are the highest in demand at schools and teens will sell the medication if they have it.

We need to recognize that not only prescription drugs are being abused. You also have teens abusing cold medicines, diet pills, laxatives, and pain relievers to get high. These are all medications that you may have in your medicine cabinet and your teen can buy over-the-counter at any pharmacy.

Teens are also throwing what is called "Pharm Parties." Pharm parties are where friends get together and each person will bring a prescription drug, then they mix all of them into a big bowl, everyone grabs a handful of random pills and they take them. They have no idea what pills they are taking but I guess that is all part of the fun for them. This kind of party can have very dangerous consequences.

It's important to pay attention to your teens slang when talking to their friends, things your teen may leave lying around their room or in their trash can, physical and behavior changes so you can properly determine if they are using prescription drugs. By simply recognizing these things you can make a conscious decision whether you need to look a little further.

 **Slang Terms used to describe Prescription Drugs:**

- Hillbilly heroin
- Oxycotton
- Barbs
- Phennies
- Yellow jackets
- Sleeping pills
- Zombie pills
- Vitamin R
- Roses
- Uppers
- Trail mix
- Oxy
- Percs
- Reds
- Tooies
- Candy
- Tranks
- Skippy
- Bennies
- Hearts
- Pharming
- Recipe
- OC
- Happy pills
- Red birds
- Yellows
- Downers
- A-minus
- The smart drug
- Black beauties
- Speed
- Pharm parties

 **Slang Terms used to describe how they feel:**

- High
- Spracked
- Gone
- Loaded
- Buzzed
- Blown

 **Paraphernalia to look for:**

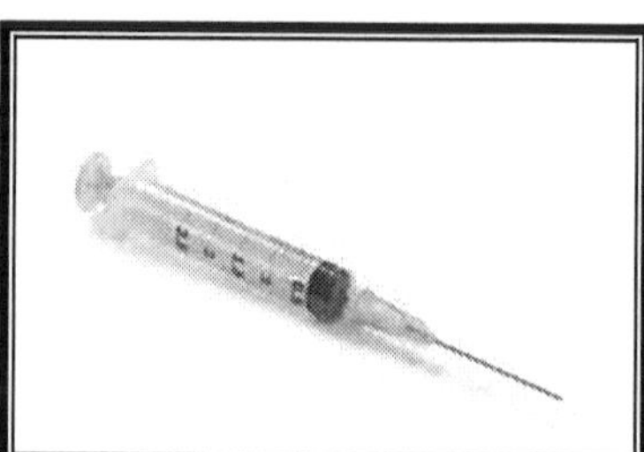

Syringe

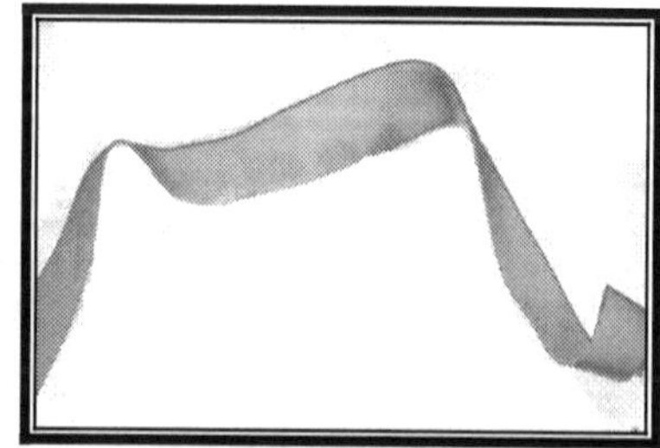

Thin rubber hose

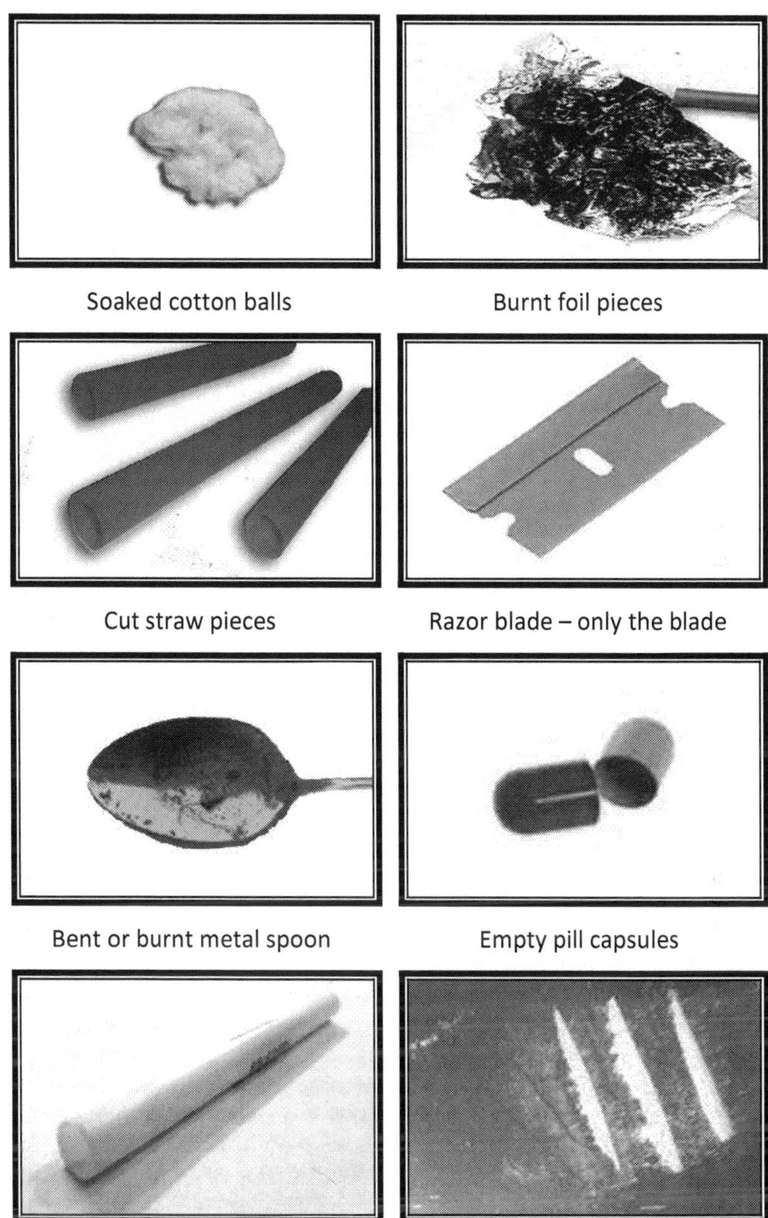

Soaked cotton balls

Burnt foil pieces

Cut straw pieces

Razor blade – only the blade

Bent or burnt metal spoon

Empty pill capsules

Hollowed out pens or markers

Mirror with white powder marks

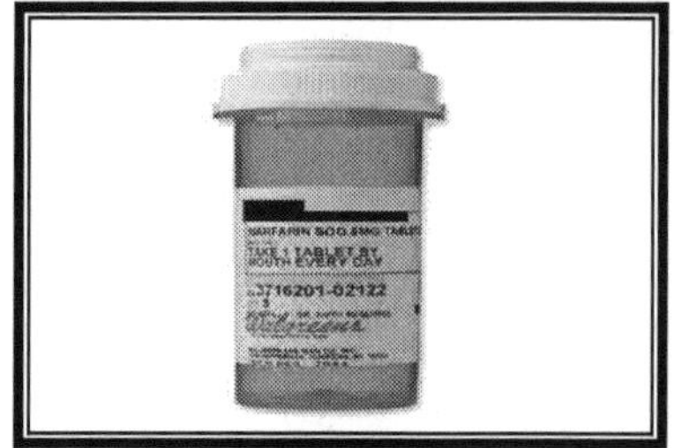

Empty medicine bottles

Rolled up dollar bills

Medicine bottles with a mixture of pills

Breath mint tin with pills inside

⚠ **Physical changes:**

When it comes to your teens physical appearance, there are a few obvious signs to look out for. Since there is such a wide variety of prescription drugs being used, the physical changes can vary depending on if they are taking a stimulant, hallucinogen or depressant. When your teen is abusing prescription drugs that are not theirs, the drug may have the opposite effect that it would have if it was used properly. For example, if your teen takes Ritalin that is not prescribed to them, rather than it calming them down it will make them jittery and give them an increased energy.

Let's start with the physical changes of your teen taking a prescription drug that is a stimulant. If they are abusing a stimulant you may notice that your teen is very jittery and kind of hyper. Stimulants give an increase in energy so they appear to be moving at a faster pace than usual and talking at a rapid speed. Their eyes may open wide and be unable to focus. And since stimulants suppress appetite, your teen may experience weight loss.

Now if your teen is taking a prescription drug that is a hallucinogen or depressant their physical changes may be slightly different. You may notice glassy and blood shot eyes. Your teen may also appear dazed and confused. They may just wander around looking lost with a slouch appearance.

 **Behavior changes:**

The most common behavior change in a teen who abuses prescription drugs is the difference in their sleep patterns. Depending on the prescription drug, they may stay awake for long periods at a time and then crash and sleep for an entire day. On the other hand, the prescription drug can have the opposite effect and they have excessive sleeping which will cause your teen to neglect their responsibilities.

From what I have seen it seems to be the stimulant drugs like Ritalin and Adderall that cause them to stay awake for long periods. Depressant drugs like pain killers Vicodin and Norco will have them dozing in and out of sleep all day long. I used to date someone who had an addiction to pain killers. He had built up such a large immune to the pain killers to the point that he was taking 20-25 pills at a time! The pills made him so sleepy that he literally slept 21 hours a day. The only time he was awake was if he was moving around. The minute he would sit or lay down, he would fall asleep. Overall he would take about 75 pills a day which I would consider a very heavy addiction.

Teens will commonly take stimulant pills to stay awake so they can study for long hours but at the same time they seem very frazzled, overly stressed out, or have major anxiety. Their brain seems scattered and they could appear dazed and confused. If they are taking drugs that are not prescribed to them then the effects could be dangerous and serious.

Prescription drug abuse is becoming extremely common among teens so it's very important for you to pay attention to the proper signs. The reality is, every teen has access to either prescription drugs or over the counter drugs in their household. And they are left out in the open and easily accessible to your teen. It may start with them taking just a few pills. When it goes unnoticed then they take more. They may even bring them to school and sell them to their classmates. My brother used to take Ritalin that was prescribed to him and sell the pills at school all the time when we were teens. Prescription drug abuse is very real. It's happening everywhere, so just don't be naïve. Teens are always looking for something that is going to give them the advantage in school, give them a heightened sensation in life or alter their frame of mind... and prescription drugs can give them that feeling.

Remember, prescription drug abuse is only a problem when your teen is using medication that is not prescribed to them, taking more than the amount prescribed to them, or taking medication that is not used for its intended purpose. When teens abuse prescription drugs it is very easy to gain an addiction and become very dependent on the drug. It doesn't take long for an addiction to grow and prescription drugs can cause long term brain injuries or even death if they aren't given help for their addiction.

You need to look beyond the obvious signs and stay in tune with your teen. Who they choose to surround themselves with, what you notice lying around their room no matter how small it may appear, along with your teens physical and/or behavior changes will all play a key role in knowing if your teen is hiding something from you. Don't be paranoid, just be aware!

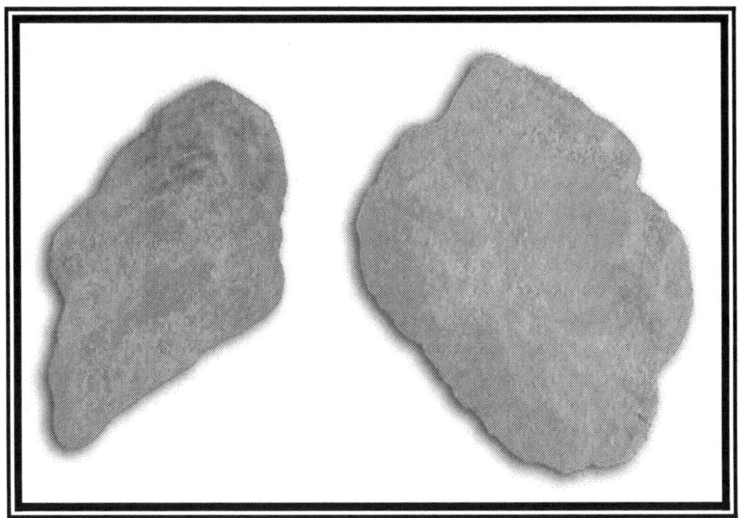

METHAMPHETAMINE

meth ◦ am ◦ phet ◦ a ◦ mine

a colorless crystalline solid, stimulant drug which causes a strong feeling of euphoria and is highly addictive

"If you can compare anything to a weapon of mass destruction on a community it's methamphetamine"

– Jack Riley

METHAMPHETAMINE

The current number of meth users are 1.6% of 8th graders. 1.3% of 10th graders, and 1.2% of 12th graders. 14% of 10th graders feel it is easy to get their hands on meth.

"Monitoring the Future (MTF) Survey"

Methamphetamine is a growing problem among teens whether we would like to admit it or not. I suffered from a meth addiction for several years and have seen some really devastating consequences. It's the devils drug as it can cause your teen to really lose themselves. A meth addiction can cause teens to steal, lie and deceive, hurt the people they love and care about the most, or even go to jail. The jails are filled with young men and woman that suffer from meth addiction. When asked at what age they first started using meth I was amazed to find out how many of them were just 15 years old.

Teens that are abusing meth will definitely surround themselves with other teens that are abusing the same drug. They will stay awake for several days before getting any sleep, find things to do to stay busy, and steal to support their expensive habit. When I used meth with my friends we would spend hours fixing something that would normally take only 30 minutes. I had friends that would steal merchandise from stores and exchange it for meth. I even had a friend stand in the middle of the street and start directing traffic.

Parents need to pay attention as their teen falls into the socialization period of their life. Teens are so easily persuaded by their peers to try anything that is going to give them a "good" feeling and meth is one of those drugs. To your teen, they don't notice the changes in their physical appearance and behavior and they don't think that their parents will notice either. If you know what to look for then you stay one step ahead of your teen.

It's important to pay attention to your teens slang when talking to their friends, things your teen may leave lying around their room or in their trash can, physical and behavior changes so you can properly determine if they are using methamphetamine. By simply recognizing these things you can make a conscious decision whether you need to look a little further.

Slang Terms used to describe Methamphetamine:

- Meth
- Speed
- Ice
- Tina
- Ish
- Dub
- Pick me up
- Fire
- 20/20
- Poison
- Shit
- Crystal
- Shards
- Juice
- Bomb
- 8 Ball
- Shiz-nick
- Boo-yah
- Hippy crack
- Nazi dope
- Tweak
- Dope
- Crystal meth
- Go fast
- Tiner
- Jet fuel
- Crank
- Pookie
- Crypto

Slang Terms used to describe how they feel:

- Tweaking balls
- Spun
- Loaded
- Wired
- On a good one
- Spun monkey
- 10/2
- Tweak mission
- Twacked out
- Toked
- Twisted
- Amped
- Cranked up
- Cloud 9
- On a sick one
- Tore up from the floor up
- Spracked
- Blown
- Lit
- Ripped
- Jacked
- Getting twisted
- Fried

Paraphernalia to look for:

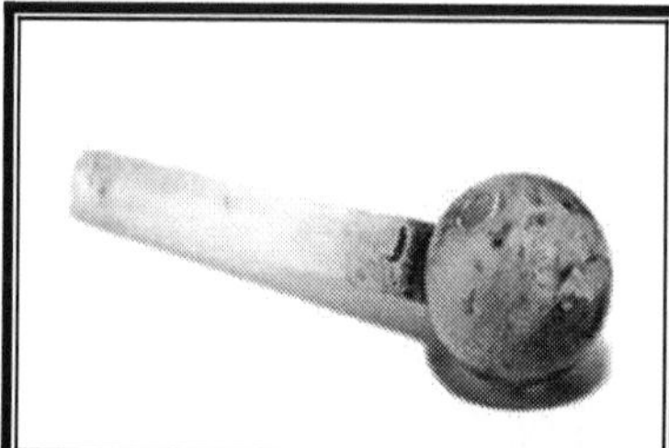

Glass pipe / Oil burner

Water bottle with hole on side

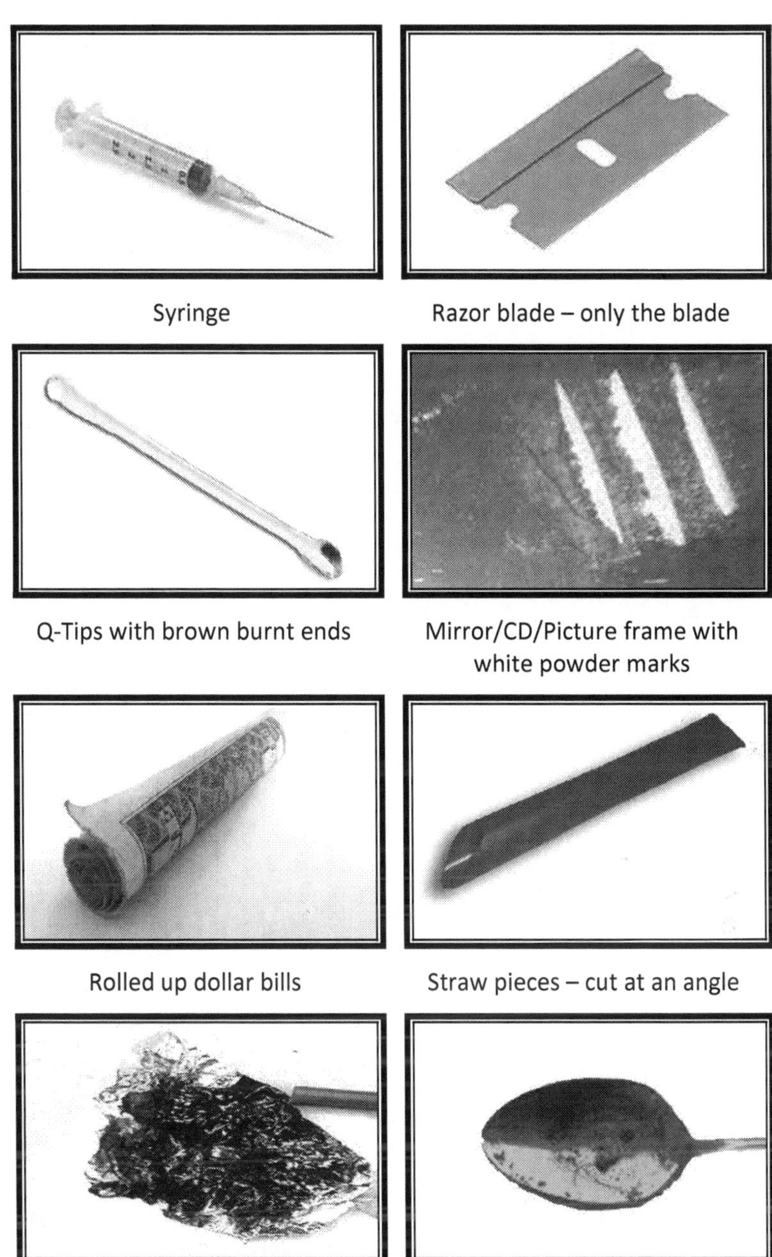

Syringe

Razor blade – only the blade

Q-Tips with brown burnt ends

Mirror/CD/Picture frame with white powder marks

Rolled up dollar bills

Straw pieces – cut at an angle

Burnt foil pieces

Bent or burnt metal spoons

Plastic baggies with white powder marks (typically have some kind of pattern on the bag)

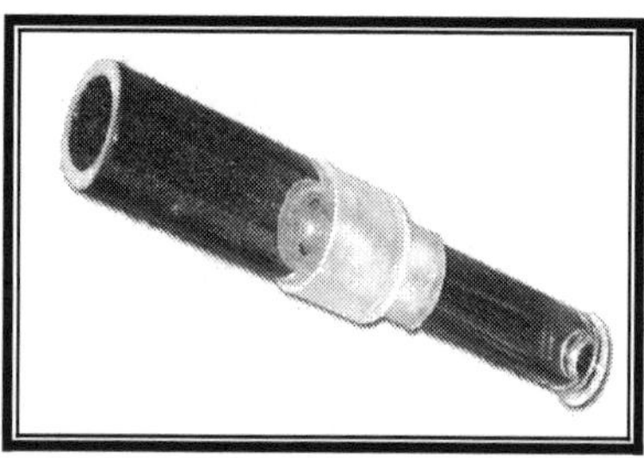
Glass pipe stems

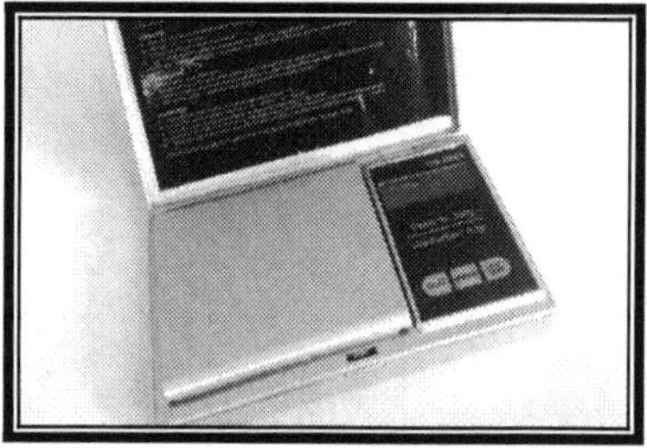
Handheld scale

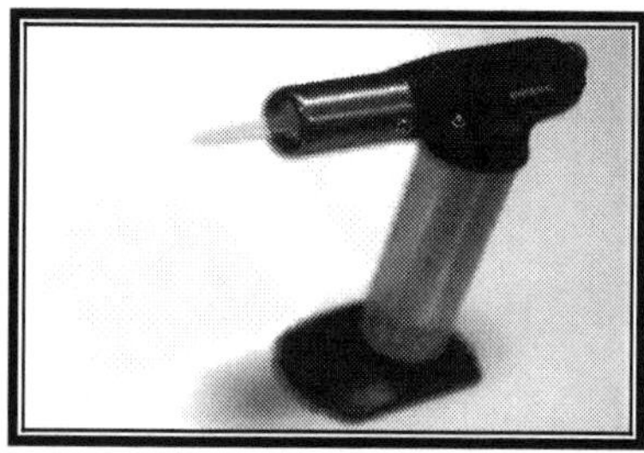
Torch lighter

Small grocery bag pieces in trash can

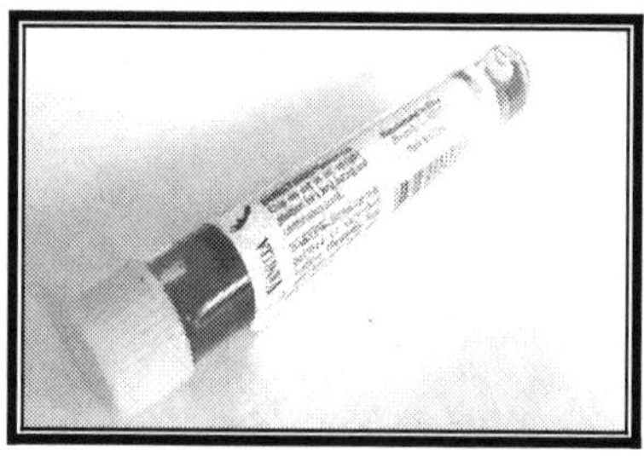
Glass tube air freshener

Portable propane tank

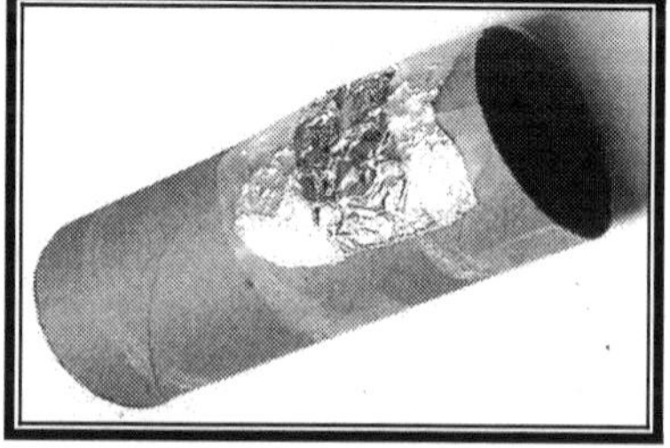
Empty toilet paper roll with foil piece on side

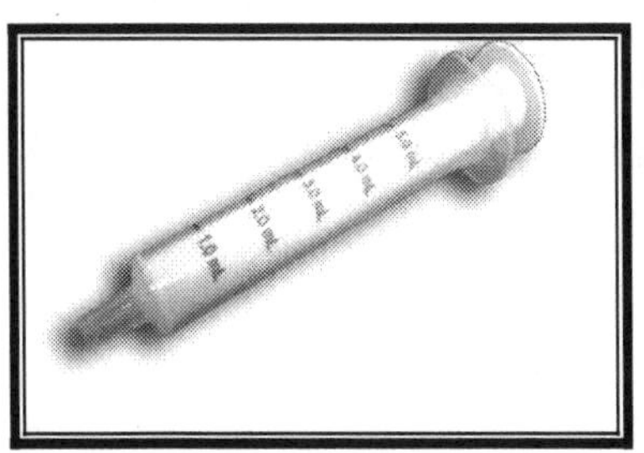

Medicine dropper

Broken light bulb

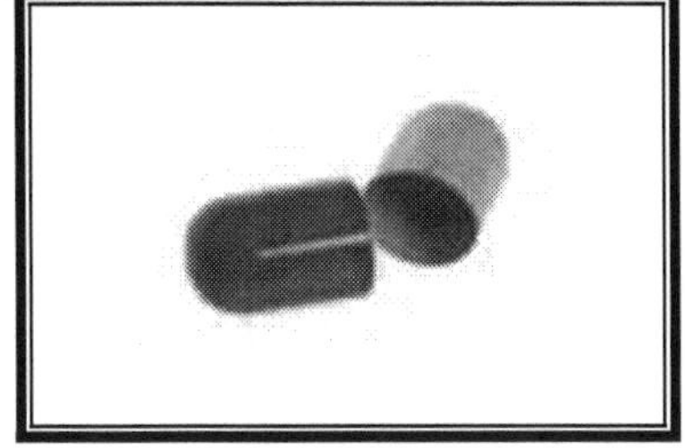

Empty pill capsules

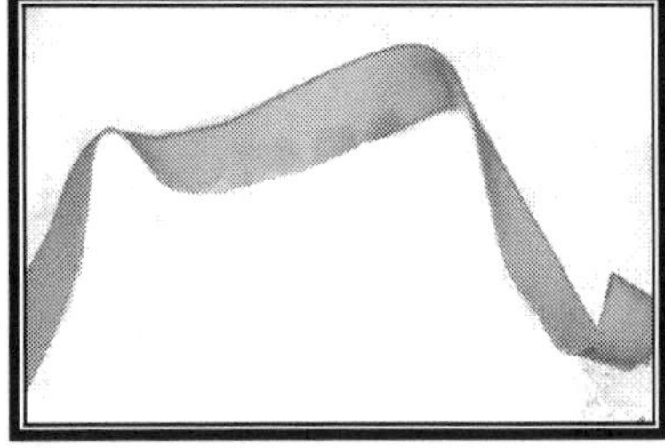

Thin rubber hose

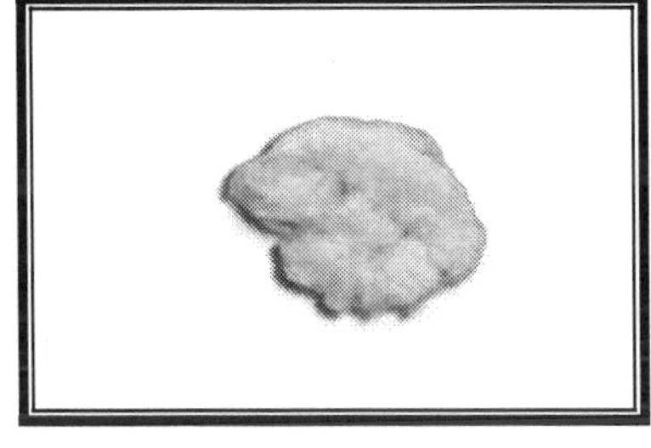

Soaked cotton balls

Burn marks on the carpet

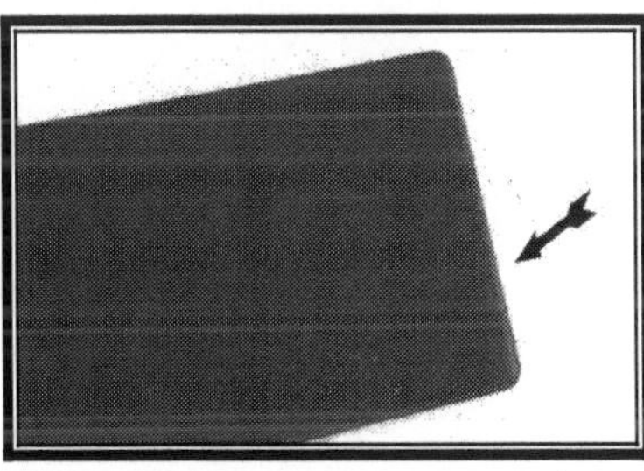

Card or driver license with white powder marks on edges

Physical changes:

When it comes to your teens physical appearance, there are a few obvious signs to look out for. An increase in acne or face and body sores is quite common among methamphetamine users because they tend to pick at their skin a lot. Weight loss and face thinning are another common sign of meth use. Meth causes a loss of appetite and usually a few days will go by before a meth user even notices that they haven't ate. When I was using meth I went from 145 pounds to 105 pounds in just a few months. I didn't even notice how skinny I had got until I saw a picture of me a few years later. You will also notice that visibly your teen appears overly alert. More alert than usual, your teen will have very wide eyes.

When a teen uses meth, they usually spend a lot of time indoors which will cause them to have a rather pale complexion. Several days may go by before your teen even goes outside. They may also wear sunglasses more often than usual, even indoors. They try to hide their eyes and have a sense that everyone is looking at them.

Your teen will also develop some poor hygiene which will also lead to tooth decay. Typically meth users are up for a few days at a time causing them to develop poor hygiene. You see, for every few days they are awake it really only feels like just one day to the user so they only brush their teeth and take a shower one time.

When you combine all of these visible changes, your teen will basically look a hot mess. Their face will appear older and a lot less attractive when you factor in the lack in hygiene, pale complexion, face thinning, and increase in acne.

Over a period of time that will start to affect a rather permanent visible change. I have several friends that have face scars, twitching, and teeth grinding problems that are all due to permanent effects of meth. I can tell if someone has once abused meth just by looking at them, even if they have not used meth in several years.

 **Behavior changes:**

The most common behavior change in a teen who uses meth is their increased alertness and change in sleep patterns. When I used meth, my friends and I would stay up for three to four days at a time, sleep for one full day, then start the cycle all over. I would stay up all day and night coloring, cleaning, playing video games, and building things… just staying busy. My mom would ask what I was doing up all night and I would just tell her that I couldn't sleep. It was a believable story to tell a mom that didn't know anything about drugs. Meth is like a long term caffeine rush.

I used to have a saying, "never have a tweaker fix anything." That saying rang true one too many times. A meth user will spend several hours trying to fix something or put something together and the end result was that they didn't fix anything. In fact they only made it worse. My friends and I spent hours putting a rather simple computer desk together and when we went to go move it, the whole thing fell apart. I also had another friend try to fix a stereo and blew the entire hotel floor's power out. They tend to stay over focused on one thing at a time but at the same time aren't really getting anything done.

The last major behavior change in a meth user is that they become untrustworthy. Stealing, whether it be money or merchandise, is extremely common. I think the most common saying is, "you can't trust a tweaker." I used to live with a meth dealer and he constantly sold to teens that were willing to steal anything in exchange for the drug. He sold to mechanics that would steal money from customers for repairs they never did, I stole tips at work so I could buy the drug, my friends would steal from their parents, the list just goes on. The fact is, when your teen is high on meth, they just don't think about their actions or who they are hurting. They will do what is needed so they can get meth since it is so highly addictive.

Some meth users, not all, will have extreme paranoia when they are high. I had a friend who sold meth and he always used to say, "give me a weekend with them and I'll have them hooked." He was able to convince someone that his girlfriend was cheating and he went over to her house and assaulted her. They think that everyone is looking at them, people are out to get them, and that people are hiding in the bush. All of these things may seem ridiculous but to a meth addict this is totally normal behavior.

Methamphetamine used to be my poison for many years so let me tell you, it's definitely a growing problem among teens and a cause for concern. I have personally experienced how methamphetamine can affect not only my personal life but the lives of my family and the people around me.

When I had a methamphetamine addiction I changed my friends, stole from my family, quit my job, and virtually gave up everything. I managed to completely change my life for the worse within just 6 months of using the drug. Methamphetamine just caused me to do some things that I would have never done if I weren't high. I have really seen the evil come out of people. I have witnessed countless people destroy their lives and hurt the people that trust them the most all over a methamphetamine addiction. I can tell you that I wish my parents knew what to look for because maybe they could have intervened in my life.

The bottom line is, if you notice that your teen is looking very alert, staying awake for several days, and seems to be doing a lot of "busy" work then you need to pay attention to that. Those are clear signs of potential methamphetamine use.

You need to look beyond the obvious signs and stay in tune with your teen. Who they choose to surround themselves with, what you notice lying around their room no matter how small it may appear, along with your teens physical and/or behavior changes will all play a key role in knowing if your teen is hiding something from you. Don't be paranoid, just be aware!

HEROIN

her ◦ o ◦ in

a white powder or brown tar like solid, derived from morphine that is a highly addictive drug

"When I look into your eyes all I can see is a soulless silhouette of a person who found happiness in being a pincushion"

– Michael Kloss

HEROIN

In 2011, 4.2 million Americans aged 12 or older (or 1.6 percent) had used heroin at least once in their lives. It is estimated that about 23 percent of individuals who used heroin become dependent on it .

"U.S. Department of Health and Human Services National Institutes of Health"

Rarely is heroin use a one-time isolated incident. Once a teen starts using heroin it is extremely hard for them to stop. You see, if your teen is using heroin on a regular basis their body will begin to depend on heroin to function properly. If they try to stop using heroin their body will go into shock. When that happens, it's very hard to watch your teen go through that.

Heroin is a far larger problem than we would like to believe. Heroin is either smoked on top of foil, or most commonly injected directly into their bloodstream. Overdosing from heroin because they either injected too much or had a bad reaction can be quite scary. It can cause your teen to be hospitalized or even result in death.

I always thought that a heroin user had a certain look to them, a messy and dirty look, maybe some missing teeth, but through my years of meeting several heroin users I was really surprised to find out that I was dead wrong! I met so many teens that were addicted to heroin and they were all so beautiful and innocent looking. They attended private schools and came from a good family. By the time the parents even realized that there may be a problem, their teen had either dropped out of school or was arrested. And all of these teens showed clear signs of heroin abuse. I am positive that if their parents would have known what to look for then they may have been able to get them help for their addiction.

It's important to pay attention to your teens slang when talking to their friends, things your teen may leave lying around their room or in their trash can, physical and behavior changes so you can properly determine if they are using heroin. By simply recognizing these things you can make a conscious decision whether you need to look a little further.

Slang Terms used to describe Heroin:

- Tar
- Heron
- Mud
- Skirts
- Skunk
- China white
- Dragon
- Black pearl
- White boy
- Scag
- Thunder
- H
- Dope
- Black tar
- Outfits
- Dr Feelgood
- Ron
- Chiba
- Scat
- Darts
- Hell dust
- Smack
- Junk
- Rigs
- Balloons
- Cheese
- Big H
- Sack
- Train
- Brown
- Girl

Slang Terms used to describe how they feel:

- Strung out
- Wasted
- Chasing the dragon
- H-ed out
- High
- Loaded
- Smacked back

 **Paraphernalia to look for:**

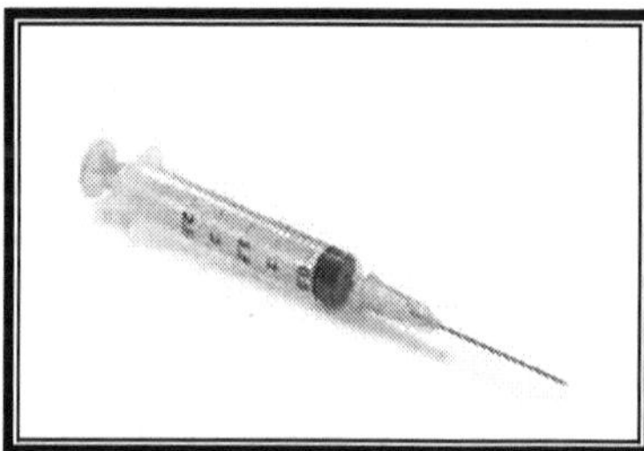

Syringe

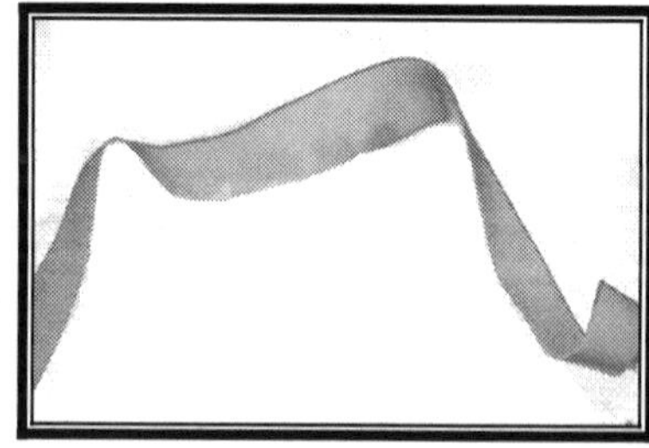

Thin rubber hose

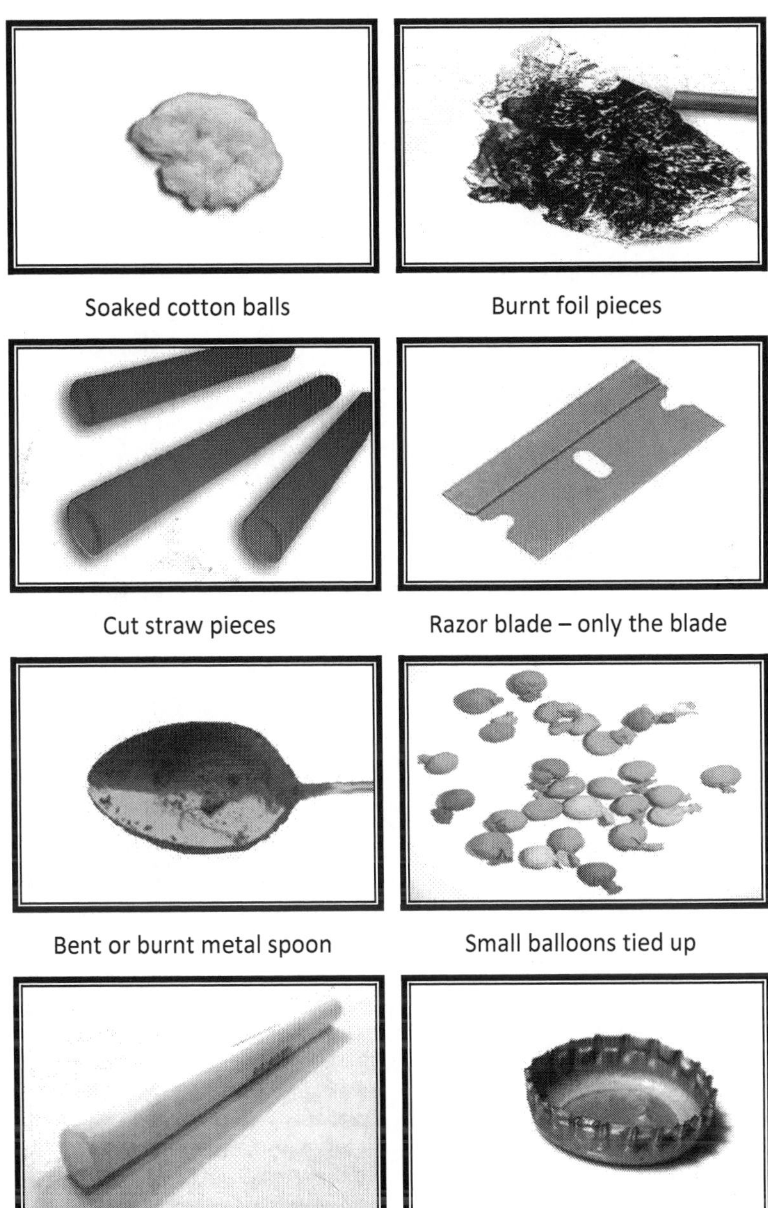

Soaked cotton balls

Burnt foil pieces

Cut straw pieces

Razor blade – only the blade

Bent or burnt metal spoon

Small balloons tied up

Hollowed out pen

Bottle caps

Soda can cut in half

Rolled up dollar bills

Tea light candle

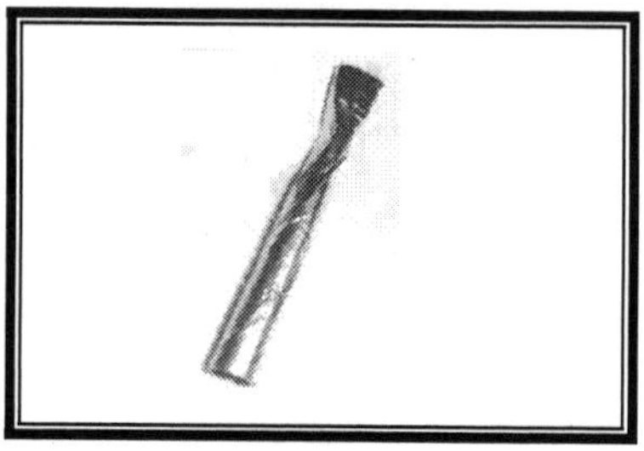

Foil rolled into straw

Foil pieces in trash can

Small grocery bag pieces in trash can

 **Physical changes:**

When it comes to your teens physical appearance, there are a few obvious signs to look out for. Tiredness seems to be the biggest excuse given for the visible change in your teen. The reason this is given as an excuse is because heroin causes eye lids to flutter, eyes roll into the back of their head, and their eyes are constantly closing. I have a close friend that has struggled with long term heroin use and when we would get together I always knew when she was high because her eyes would constantly flutter closed and she looked like she was struggling to stay awake.

Since heroin is most commonly injected directly into a visible vein, broken veins otherwise known as track marks, are the classic sign of a heroin user. Heroin cannot be injected into the same vein too many times so a teen will have multiple broken veins. These broken veins are most commonly found on the top of the forearm and in between toes. Teens will try to hide their track marks so they use areas that are easy to cover up.

Face and body acne are extremely common as well. You will notice an increase in face acne and body acne that usually appears on the top of the arms and back. Heroin can cause a teen to be a "picker," meaning they will pick at their face causing sores and scabs. The scabs are extremely visible and usually on the face and arms.

⚠ **Behavior changes:**

The obvious sign of your teen using heroin is nodding off and falling asleep. I had a friend that would literally fall asleep whether it was at my kitchen table or in his car before he could even get to my front door. It's important to recognize the difference between the typical nodding off that teens will do when they are tired and nodding off due to heroin use. Once a teen uses heroin, the high is so intense that it will cause them to nod off… no matter where they are. Their eyes will roll into the back of their head, the eye lids flutter, and they will consistently nod off and on. Your teen could be sitting on the couch having a conversation with you and in a split second be nodding off in the middle of you talking. Heroin is very powerful.

Another common behavior change is being withdrawn from family. They may also change their friends and start hanging out with other people who are also using heroin. You need to understand, they feel that people who don't use heroin don't understand them (and so to speak that would be true). So in order to hide their heroin addiction they just withdraw from those who care about them the most and surround themselves with other users who are just like them.

Heroin users are unable to hold a steady job due to their inability to function properly. Heroin just makes them incoherent and lazy. Once they develop a serious addiction to heroin, they cannot function without it. They have to use heroin to appear somewhat "normal" because without it they would break into a sweat, become very sick and have the jitters all day.

Heroin users become very untrustworthy. Because heroin can be expensive, they tend to steal so they can support their addiction. They will often steal from their family, retail stores, friends, and basically anyone they can. I would estimate that the typical amount spent on heroin by a single person is about $80 a day. Other than stealing they will borrow money and lie about what it is for. They will borrow money from their parents to go out with their friends and instead of actually going somewhere they will spend that money on drugs. Think about it, if your teen is using heroin, where did they get the money to pay for it? Most likely from you unless they have a job.

Heroin is like the devil in disguise. The most ordinary teen can be addicted to heroin. I knew several teens from a upper class private school who used heroin on a daily basis. I have also seen young girls go from never doing a single drug to becoming totally addicted to heroin and the damage that it had caused. My point is, don't think that because you have done everything right as a parent, your teen can't become addicted to heroin. The fact is, it's out there and it's very accessible to your teen. It's more common than we would like to think. I have seen it happen over and over again and it breaks my heart.

If your teen is constantly dozing off at random places like the kitchen table or while sitting up and you see broken veins on their arms, your teen is most likely using heroin and it's worth looking into. I can tell you from personal experience that it is very rare that a teen only uses heroin once. Heroin is probably one of the most addictive drugs out there.

You need to look beyond the obvious signs and stay in tune with your teen. Who they choose to surround themselves with, what you notice lying around their room no matter how small it may appear, along with your teens physical and/or behavior changes will all play a key role in knowing if your teen is hiding something from you. Don't be paranoid, just be aware!

COCAINE

co ◦ caine

a stimulant: an addictive drug obtained from the leaves of the coca plant, has euphoric and numbing properties

"Cocaine made people deaf, it made people dead and it made people real obnoxious"

– Linda Ronstadt

COCAINE

In 2011, 14.3 percent of American's have tried cocaine ages 12 and older, with 6 percent having tried it by their senior year of high school.

"National Institute on Drug Abuse"

Cocaine is widely considered the "Rich Man's Drug" because a person will typically spend $80-100 per day. Cocaine is typically ingested by snorting through the nose, rubbing along the gums in the mouth or private areas. It causes the senses to become intensified and produce a numbing and arousing sensation to the user making it highly addictive. Cocaine is generally used frequently since the effects only last about 30 minutes.

Cocaine is not the most common addiction among teens but it's important to realize that it does exist. For cocaine use, don't expect some dramatic change in your teen because it probably isn't going to happen. I will tell you the most noticeable physical and behavior change so it will make it easier to notice if your teen may be using cocaine. It's out there and it's not hard to get if you know the right person. Your teen is more likely to be exposed to cocaine at a party rather than anywhere else.

It's important to pay attention to your teens slang when talking to their friends, things your teen may leave lying around their room or in their trash can, physical and behavior changes so you can properly determine if they are using cocaine. By simply recognizing these things you can make a conscious decision whether you need to look a little further.

Slang Terms used to describe Cocaine:

- Blow
- Coca
- Base
- Scarface
- Rock
- White dragon
- Snow
- Dream
- Booster
- Aspirin
- All-American drug
- Soft
- Flave
- Toot
- Basuco
- Cork the air
- Coke
- Yeyo
- Bump
- Rich Man drug
- Candy
- Zip
- Candy sticks
- 51
- Her
- Candy sugar
- Devils Dandruff
- Shake
- Space
- Pariba
- Cracker jacks
- Coke-i-e-na
- Powder
- Charlie
- Cocoa puffs
- Bedrock
- Foo-foo dust
- Uptown
- Primos
- King's habit
- Aunt Nora
- Tardust witch
- Fast white lady
- Speedball
- Bah-say
- Puffer

Slang Terms used to describe how they feel:

- Blowed
- Cracked out
- Ghostbusting
- Amped
- Chalked up
- Scotty
- Beaming
- Weightless

 **Paraphernalia to look for:**

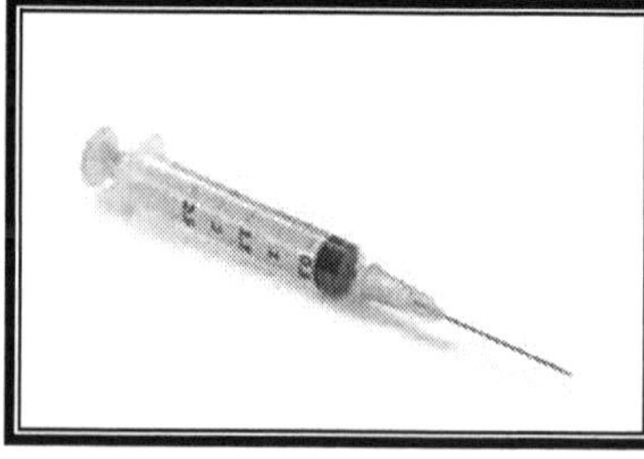

Syringe

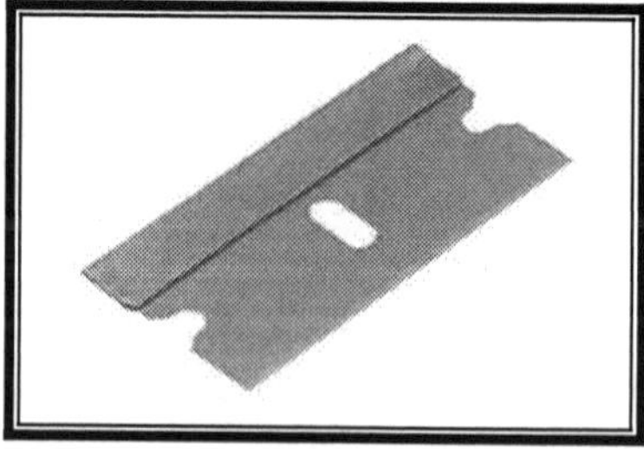

Razor blade – only the blade

Rolled up dollar bill

Cut straw pieces

Metal Brillo pads

Baking soda

Plastic baggies with white powder marks

Hand mirror with white powder marks

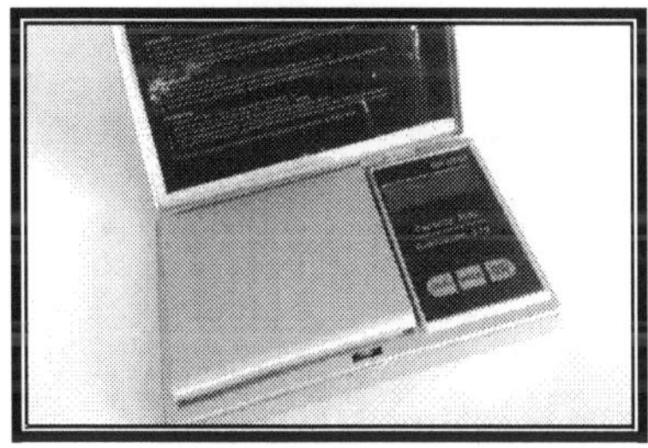

Handheld scale

Sink drain screens

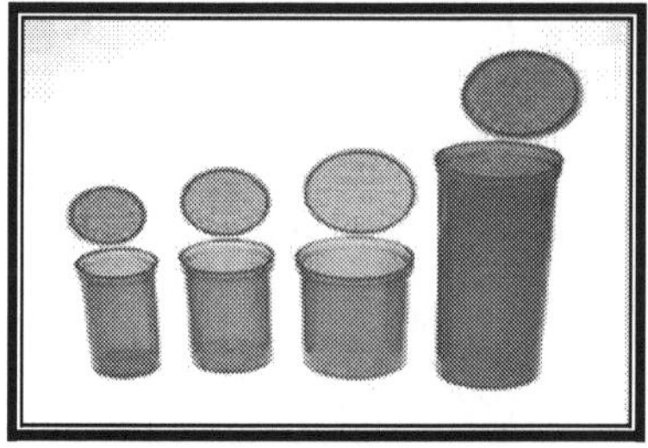

Prescription medicine bottles

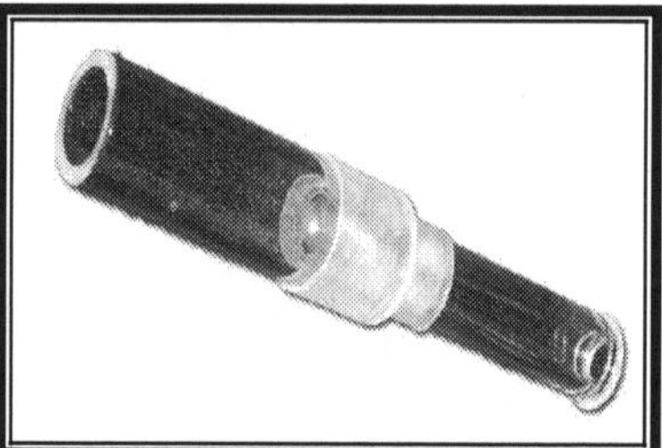

Glass pipe stems

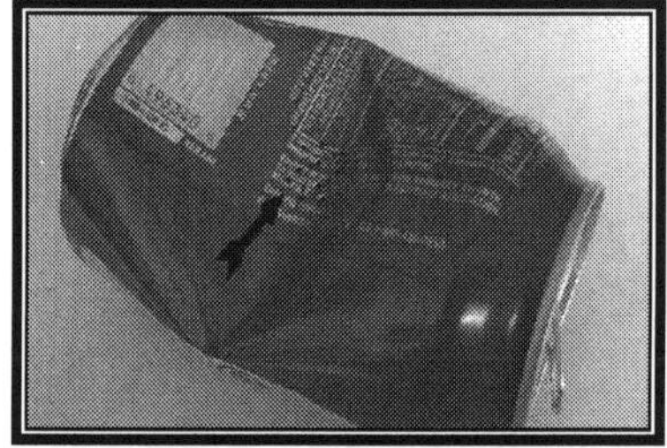

Empty soda can with pin holes on the side

Bottle caps

Broken light bulb

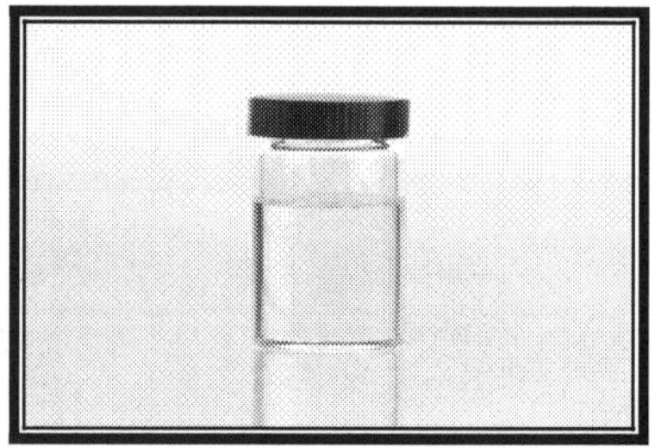

Small vials

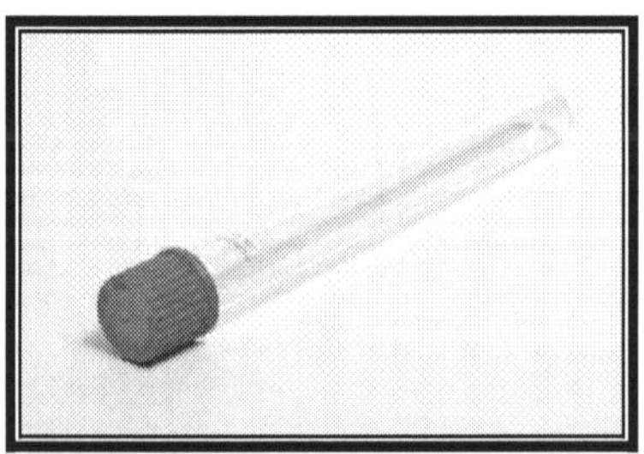

Small or large glass tubes

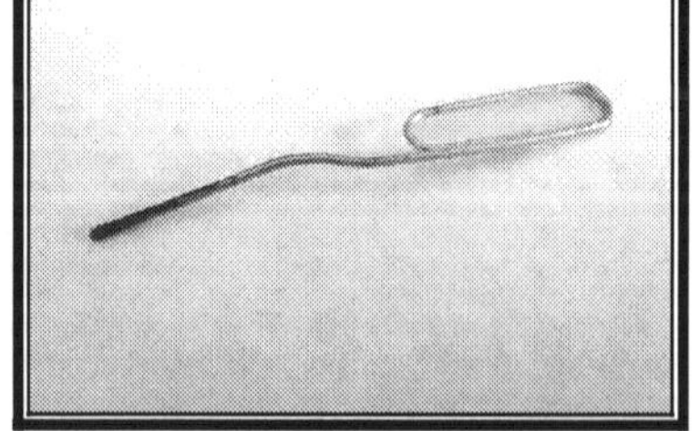

Straightened paper clips

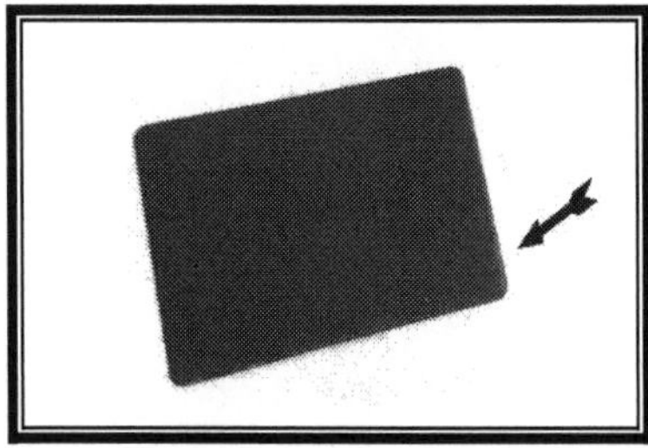

Card or driver license with white powder marks on edges

Water bottle with hole on the side

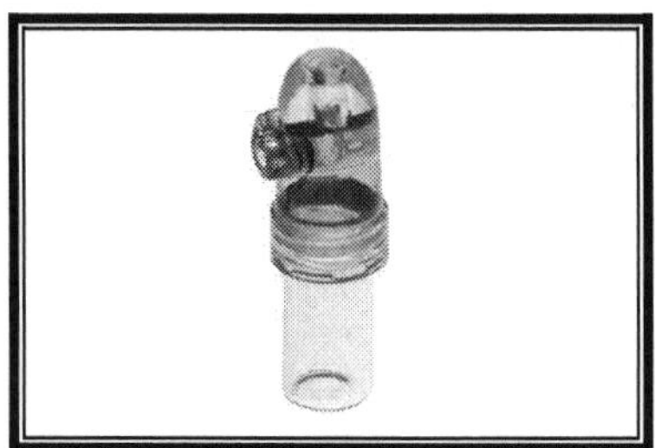

Snuff Bullet

Physical changes:

When it comes to your teens physical appearance, there are a few obvious signs to look out for. Cocaine is most commonly ingested by snorting which creates a breakdown of the cartilage in their face and nose causing it to thin out. You will notice face thinning and a runny nose or sniffling due to the cartilage breakdown. When I was about 16 I had a friend who could completely flatten his nose due to the loss of cartilage cocaine had caused. Face thinning is more of a permanent effect of cocaine use since it is caused by cartilage loss and not loss of appetite.

Cocaine is also frequently rubbed on the gums in their mouth so tooth decay is unavoidable. It doesn't happen overnight, however if their mouth hygiene isn't the best and they also combine the cocaine to the gum lines constantly, I think you can see why there may be decay. Cocaine can cause a teen to become extremely lazy and tired since they are numbing themselves so a lack of hygiene is bound to occur. You may also notice that your teen has a slurred and rapid speech due to cocaine use.

Body shaking can also be an affect of cocaine use, however in my experience I have only seen this physical change in someone who is going through withdrawal.

 **Behavior changes:**

Because cocaine heightens the senses, your teens behavior will change to maximize the sensation of those feelings. Their performance at school will change with their inability to focus and lack of concentration. Typically teens will just stop going to school all together. I wouldn't say that cocaine causes your teen to change their friends because the likeliness of them trying cocaine with their friends for the first time is highly probable. If your teen is introduced to cocaine it will likely be from one of their friends.

Cocaine can become a rather expensive addiction. Your teen will start to steal or deceive their family and friends to get the money to pay for it. Typical chore or allowance money isn't going to be enough to pay for cocaine. They may lie about going to the movies or out with friends and use the money you give them to buy cocaine instead. If several of their friends also use cocaine then they may all pitch in some money and buy a larger amount to share. Cocaine can cause a lot of deception between hiding their addiction and coming up with the money to pay for it.

You may also notice a change in their motivation. The activities they used to enjoy doing, they don't really enjoy anymore. Since cocaine causes a loss of coordination and laziness, they will drop out of sports or school clubs and seem withdrawn from regular activities and family. They will spend a large amount of time in their room where they have the privacy to use the cocaine at their leisure.

Cocaine can have adverse effects on your teen because it is used on a constant basis to maintain the euphoria they experience. Even though cocaine abuse isn't as common amongst teens it does exist, and if they don't abuse cocaine when they are a teen it may happen when they are a young adult. There are two types of cocaine users, your everyday users and your occasional users. Most people I know do not abuse cocaine on a daily basis but if it is offered to them they will do it.

Rarely do teens use cocaine by themselves either. It is usually used within their group of friends. When I went to school it was to my amazement that the popular crowd were cocaine users. Cocaine is often found at parties your teen will attend with friends. I have been to numerous parties and have seen firsthand dozens of teens use cocaine when it was available. Because cocaine is a rather short term high compared to most drugs a teen may use cocaine and appear completely normal an hour later. It's the physical and behavior changes that will occur over a period of time that will let you know if there may be a problem.

You need to look beyond the obvious signs and stay in tune with your teen. Who they choose to surround themselves with, what you notice lying around their room no matter how small it may appear, along with your teens physical and/or behavior changes will all play a key role in knowing if your teen is hiding something from you. Don't be paranoid, just be aware!

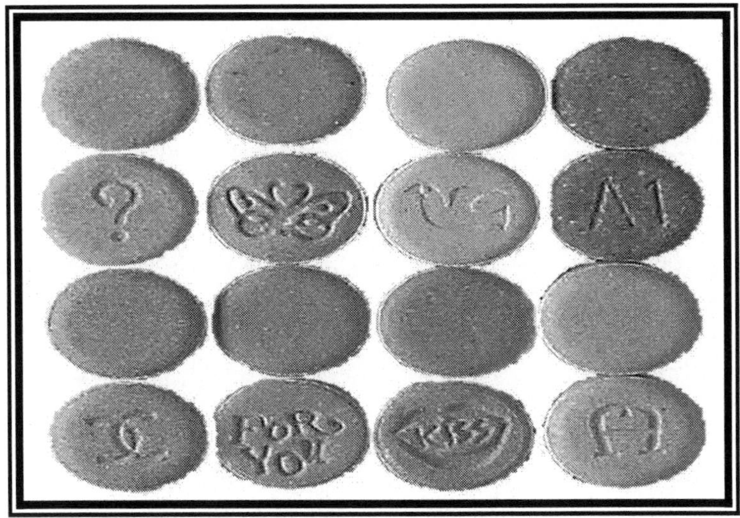

ECSTASY

ec ◦ sta ◦ sy

a recreational hallucinogenic drug: a sudden and intense feeling or emotion, mental transport or rapture from the observation of heavenly things

"Who's a better salesman, you or the drug dealer?"

– Michael Stevenson

ECSTASY

In 2011, 2.4 percent of American's ages 12-17 and 12.3 percent of American's ages 18-25 have reported using Ecstasy.

"National Survey of Drug Use and Health"

Ecstasy is a drug commonly used amongst friends at house parties, rave parties, and other events. I would describe ecstasy as methamphetamine and acid all rolled into a single pill. Ecstasy pills come in a variety of colors with different symbols on top. There are dozens of different ecstasy pills available.

Ecstasy can create an extreme sexual euphoria and give your teen warm fuzzy feelings towards other people. There is the saying, "if you have sex a few times on ecstasy, sex will never feel the same again." I think they say that because the sense of touch is intensified way more than normal. Let me make one thing clear, I mention sex because let's face the facts, the growing amount of teens experimenting with sex is on the rise. Even something simple like running water over their arms and face will feel extra good.

When I was a teen my friends and I would all do ecstasy together and when we would start to feel the effects we would give each other massages, drive in the car so we could feel the wind on our face, and just rub soft stuffed animals on our bodies because we liked the feeling. Strange? Of course it is but that's what ecstasy does.

It's important to pay attention to your teens slang when talking to their friends, things your teen may leave lying around their room or in their trash can, physical and behavior changes so you can properly determine if they are using ecstasy. By simply recognizing these things you can make a conscious decision whether you need to look a little further.

Slang Terms used to describe Ecstasy:

- X
- Adam
- Dancing shoes
- Hug drug
- Egg rolls
- Stacks
- Smartees
- Thiz
- Vowels
- Triangles
- Smurfs
- Molly
- E
- Candy
- E-bomb
- Disco biscuits
- Love drug
- Red devils
- Sweets
- Vitamin E
- 69s
- Candy raver
- Triple stacks
- Double stacks
- XTC
- Beans
- Happy pill
- Doves
- Malcolm X
- Scooby snacks
- Skittles
- Vitamin X
- Buddah
- Cloud 9
- Ice

Slang Terms used to describe how they feel:

- Rolling
- Double drop
- Tripping out
- E-tard
- Dropping
- Flipping
- Raving

Paraphernalia to look for:

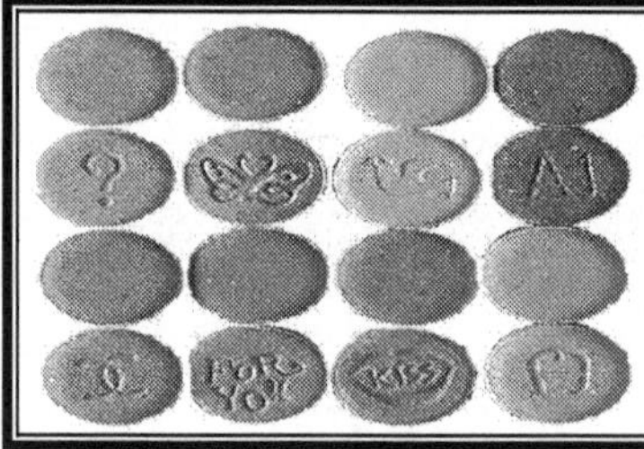

Thick pills with a symbol on top (e.g. elephant, buddah, pyramid, sun, superman logo, etc)

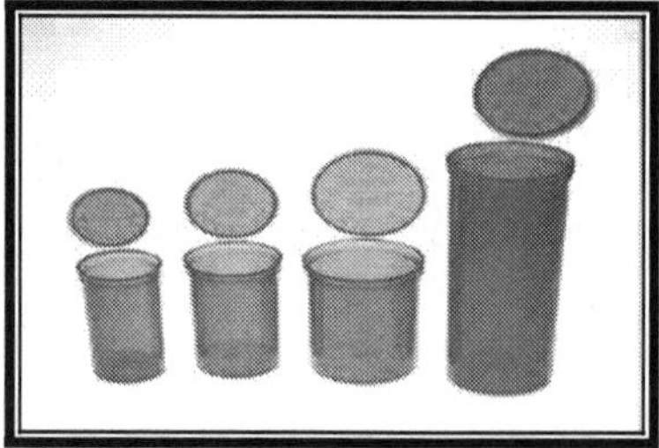

Medicine bottles with no label

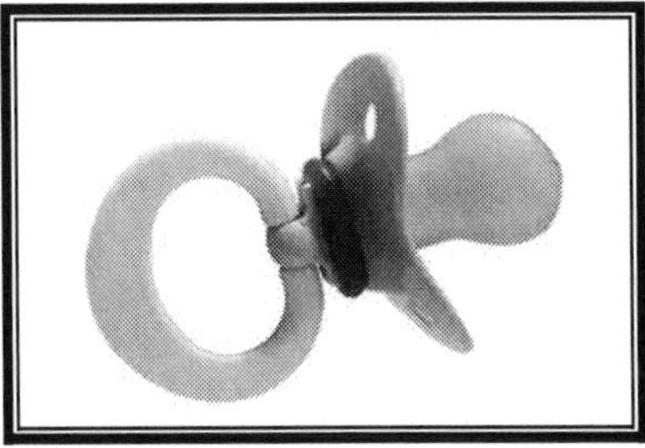

Pacifiers (typically on a bright colored beaded necklace)

Bright colored beaded bracelets and necklaces

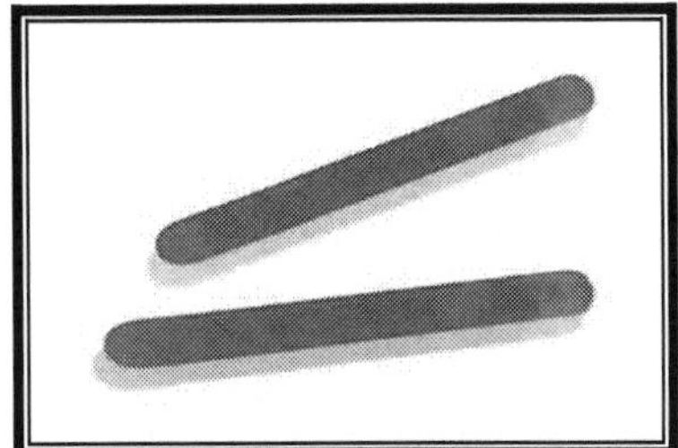

Glow sticks

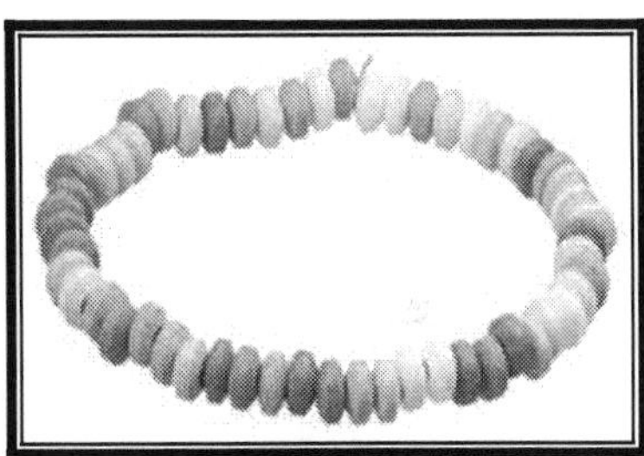

Candy necklaces

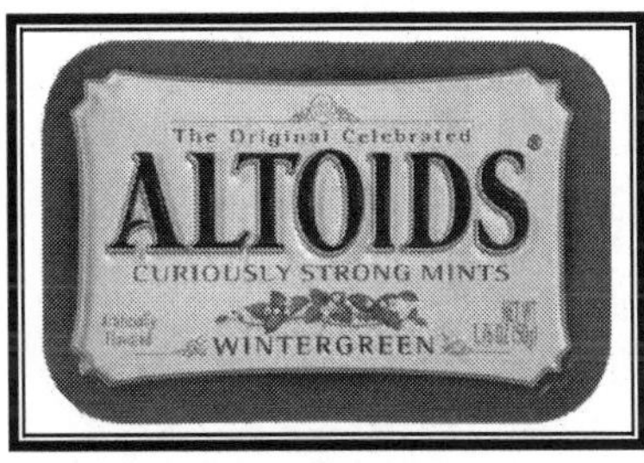

Breath mint tin with pills inside

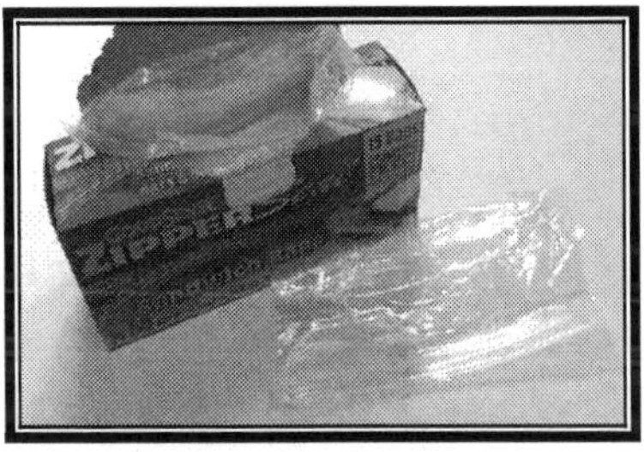

Small plastic baggies

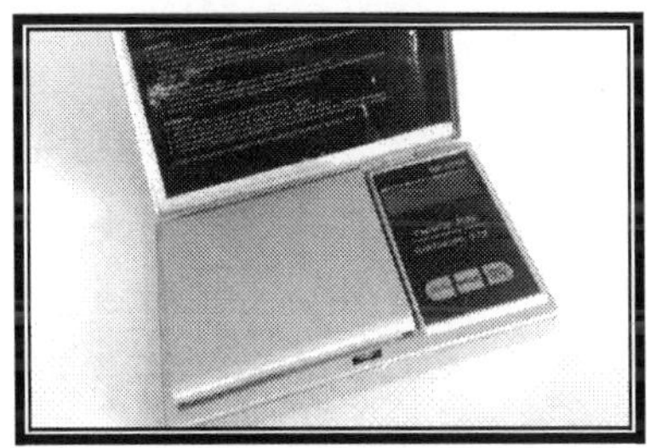

Handheld scales

Soft stuffed animals and toys

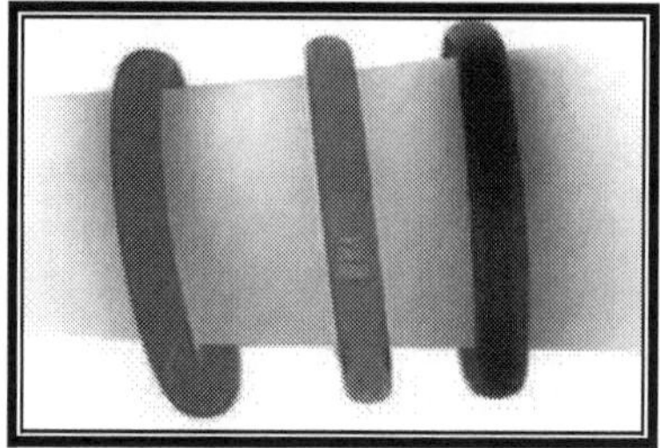

Glow Bracelets

Physical changes:

When it comes to your teens physical appearance, there are a few obvious signs to look out for. Teeth grinding and jaw clenching are super common effects of ecstasy. Teens will chew on a pacifier or gum to satisfy the grinding. When my friends and I attended a rave party and used ecstasy I can remember that we chewed on pacifiers the entire night and even on the way home the next morning. It was crazy but it felt normal at the time.

Dry mouth and even vomiting are also common physical changes. They will drink lots and lots of water while they are high to try and mask their dry mouth. The problem is, no matter how much water they drink their mouth will seem to stay dry. When I took too much ecstasy and acid together at one time I was vomiting profusely before even getting into the rave I was going to. It was awful.

A common aftereffect of ecstasy is fatigue. Your teen is usually tired from excessive body movement like dancing all night. They may have a pale complexion in the days to follow because of the lack of sun exposure they receive from staying indoors.

Behavior changes:

Your teen will suddenly have a positive upbeat mood change (more so than usual). They become very happy, loving, affectionate, the works. Everything seems to be positive, fuzzy, and loving feelings. Ecstasy definitely gives your teen an increased sense of intimacy on top of that. And I don't just mean sexually, but rubbing, lightly touching, and other physical activity will feel extra good.

Something about ecstasy also gives your teen an increased dancing sensation. Frequently used in clubs and at parties, if your teen is using ecstasy they may dance for long periods of time. I think it's because ecstasy heightens their sense of sound and touch. When using ecstasy, loud music seems to motivate their energy. They will listen to electronic dance music like techno or trance since it has a lot of digitally synthesized instruments.

When I went to a rave I was among the nicest group of people I have ever met. You could tell that they were on ecstasy because everyone was so friendly and loving. By the end of the night they were laying on the ground either sleeping or just rubbing on each other's arms, and all around looked like they have been up all night.

Basically, if you notice that your teen is up all night, frequently attending rave parties, suddenly listening to electronic dance music like techno or trace, appears to be extra happy and loving at times and exhausted at others, there is a possibility that they could be experimenting with ecstasy.

Overall ecstasy is not really a drug that is used all the time. It's really a drug used among friends and at parties but can have deadly consequences. The effects of ecstasy depend largely on the attitude and mindset of the person taking the drug at the moment. If your teen is depressed or sad and takes ecstasy, they can have a bad experience which can send them to the hospital or have them do something they wouldn't typically do. If they use ecstasy when they are happy and upbeat then they can have what is considered a good experience. I have known people to take ecstasy one time and overdose from it.

When you are a teen you don't worry about the consequences of anything you do. You care about what the drug can do to your state of mind more than anything else. Have people taken ecstasy and died from it after only taking it one time? Yes! Have people had bad experiences from ecstasy? Yes! Do teens think about any of that before taking a drug? Probably not! It's just a reality. Does that mean that you failed as a parent? Absolutely not! No matter how well you raise your teen to make good choices, the fact is, they may make a bad choice. All we can do as parents is make sure that we are aware of any behavior changes that are not normal.

You need to look beyond the obvious signs and stay in tune with your teen. Who they choose to surround themselves with, what you notice lying around their room no matter how small it may appear, along with your teens physical and/or behavior changes will all play a key role in knowing if your teen is hiding something from you. Don't be paranoid, just be aware!

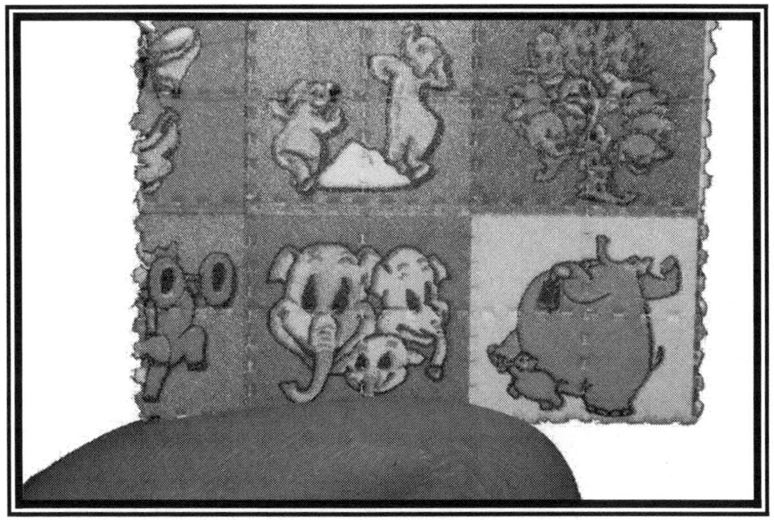

ACID

ac ◦ id

a recreational hallucinogenic drug: derived from a parasitic fungus that grows on rye, psychoactive properties when ingested

"If you've never seen an elephant ski, you've never been on acid."

– Eddie Izzard

ACID

In 2008, 1.9 percent of 8th graders, 2.6 percent of 10th graders, and 4.0 percent of 12th graders reported using LSD in their lifetime.

"Monitoring the Future (MTF) Survey"

Acid, also known as LSD, is widely known as the party drug since it is most often used at house and rave parties. Because acid is fairly inexpensive and a strong hallucinogen, acid is commonly used by a group of teens together versus all by themselves. Acid typically comes in four forms; a clear liquid, blotter paper (paper that is perforated into small squares, usually colored or have images printed on them), sugar cubes, and gel capsules.

Since acid is rarely used on a daily basis I wouldn't consider this drug to be highly addictive. Instead it becomes something fun to do amongst friends. It doesn't make this drug any less dangerous but it can make the physical and behavior changes a little harder to spot. In this case, you need to be aware of your teens physical appearance and behavior changes right after a long night out with friends.

It's important to pay attention to your teens slang when talking to their friends, things your teen may leave lying around their room or in their trash can, physical and behavior changes so you can properly determine if they are using acid. By simply recognizing these things you can make a conscious decision whether you need to look a little further.

Slang Terms used to describe Acid:

- Cid
- L
- Mellow yellow
- Sugar
- Boomers
- Doses
- The goose drop
- White Lightening
- Window pane
- Laughing gas
- Tab
- Looney toons
- Dots
- Back breaker
- Elvis
- Hippie
- Trip
- Rainbow skittles
- Dome
- Lucy in the sky w/ diamonds
- Hit
- Purple haze
- Alice
- Battery acid
- Superman
- Zen
- Blotter
- Electric Kool-aid
- Paper

Slang Terms used to describe how they feel:

- Acid trip
- Dropping
- Tripping out
- Raving
- Flipping
- Tripping out

Paraphernalia to look for:

Blotter paper (paper that is perforated into small squares, usually colored or have images printed on them)

Breath mint or eye drop bottles with a cloudy liquid

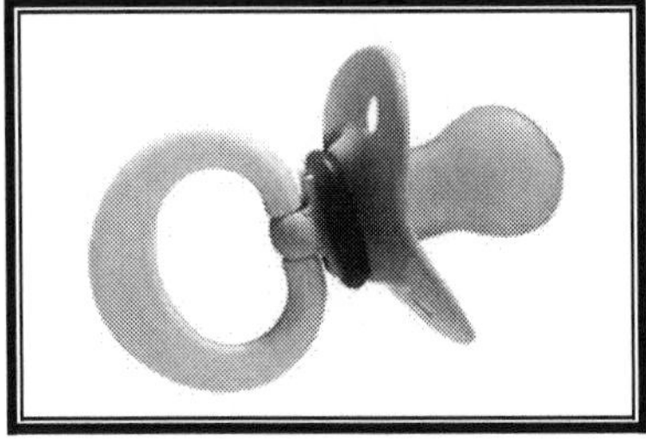

Pacifiers (typically on a bright colored beaded necklace)

Strobe light

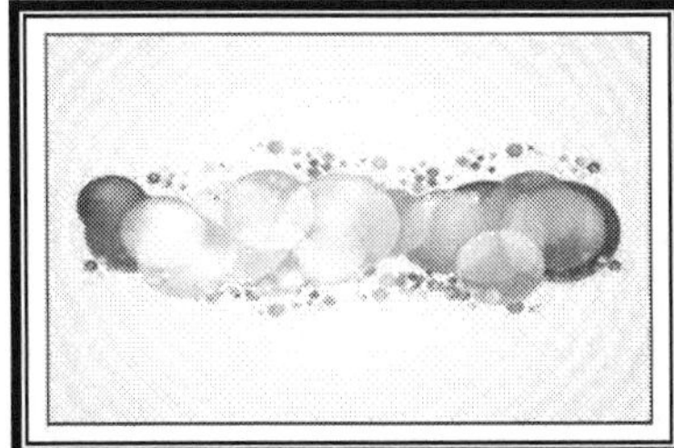

Bright colored posters

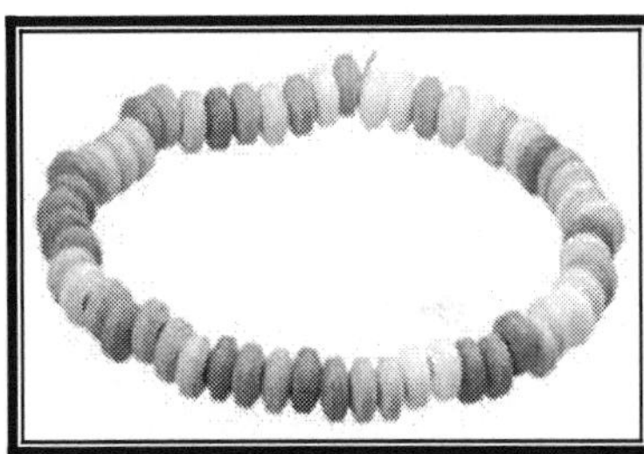

Candy necklaces

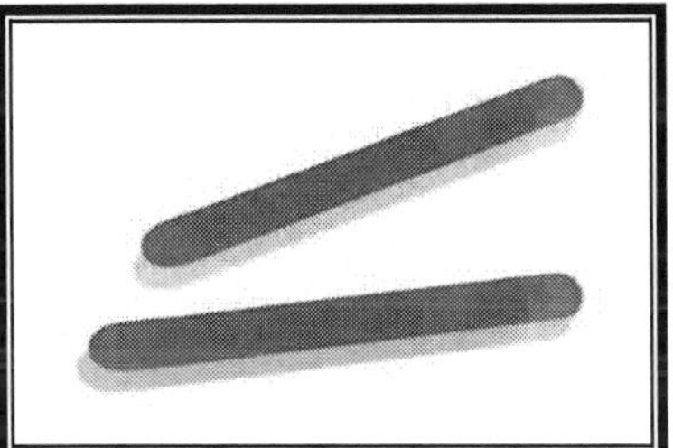

Glow sticks

Bright colored beaded bracelets and necklaces

 **Physical changes:**

When it comes to your teens physical appearance, there are a few obvious signs to look out for. When a teen uses acid they will have dilated pupils and blood shot eyes. They will appear to be wide awake and their eyes sort of wandering around since their light sensitivity is affected.

Dry mouth and teeth grinding are also very common when high on acid. They will drink an increased amount of water and use a pacifier to help with the teeth grinding. Their body temperature also rises so sweating is not uncommon and you may notice your teen wearing a tank top when its cold outside.

Since acid is mainly used in the party scene and not so much as a daily drug, you may not notice these physical changes every day. You will notice these changes more so when your teen comes back from a party or a long night out with friends.

Behavior changes:

The most common behavior change when a teen is using acid is the change in activities and music that they listen to. Acid is very popular at rave parties. And believe me when I tell you, more than 80% of the people attending a rave party are high on acid.

The loud sound of music and bright lights are extremely intense. Since acid enhances the experience of music, a teen will be listening to rave music (techno, trance, and/or indie) because it is so loud. Acid also highly affects their visual stimulation to bright colors so they may use strobe lights, black lights, and glow sticks to enhance their experience. When I was a teen I used acid with several friends and we just sat and stared at a strobe light for hours because we swore that we could see pink elephants and blue giraffes. Acid is a powerful hallucinogen and the bright flashing lights will enhance the visual delusions. On occasion they can experience paranoia which we would refer to as a "bad trip". That means that they may believe that they are being watched, chased, or even conspired against. I had a friend who thought that someone was hiding in the bush outside and that his poster was talking to him. He actually had an entire conversation with his poster.

The sense of touch is also very stimulated when on acid so you may find your teen taking extended showers or rubbing their hands and face against soft and fuzzy objects. When someone is high on acid it seems like everything they touch feels good. My friends and I would just sit around and give each other massages and rub stuffed animals on our arms. Strange, yes. But the reality is that when a person is high on acid they will do these things to maximize the experience that they have.

The National Survey on Drug Use and Health reports that 9.7 percent (more than 200,000 people) above the age of 12 have used acid for the first time each year. Even though that technically isn't a large statistic, it's a cause for major concern because it's my belief that that statistic should be much higher.

Although acid is mainly used by teens as a "fun" drug, the amount that teens tend to take at one time can be dangerous. When I would go out with my friends to rave parties, we would take several drops of acid at a time to increase the feeling. I had a friend who had taken too much at one time and had to go to the hospital because she overdosed. It was very scary.

You would be amazed at the amount of teens that are willing to try a drug, no matter what it is, when they are at a party or with friends. Acid is becoming more common in the party scene than we would like to believe so by knowing what to look for you can intervene.

You need to look beyond the obvious signs and stay in tune with your teen. Who they choose to surround themselves with, what you notice lying around their room no matter how small it may appear, along with your teens physical and/or behavior changes will all play a key role in knowing if your teen is hiding something from you. Don't be paranoid, just be aware!

SPICE

spice

also known as synthetic marijuana, a drug created by spraying herbs with synthetic chemicals

"Drugs are a bet with the mind" – Jim Morrison

SPICE

In 2012, nearly twice as many male 12th graders reported past-year use of synthetic marijuana as females in the same age group.

"Drugabuse.gov"

In recent years studies have shown a huge increase in the amount of teens using spice which is otherwise known as synthetic marijuana. According to Drugabuse.gov, of the illicit drugs most used by high-school seniors, Spice is second only to marijuana. Spice is legal in the United States and can be purchased at most tobacco shops and gas stations. Spice is known as the "teen friendly drug" because it is easy to get, considered legal, and schools and sports teams don't test for spice. Spice is most commonly smoked out of a pipe or rolled in papers and some teens are even brewing it in tea.

The reason spice is considered dangerous is because there are several chemical components and other ingredients unknown to the user and are not meant for human consumption. Although some states have recently outlawed a few of the chemicals used in spice, it is still very easy for a teen to obtain. Spice is labeled as a "safe and legal" alternative to other drugs, making it even more appealing to teens and young adults.

It's important to pay attention to your teens slang when talking to their friends, things your teen may leave lying around their room or in their trash can, physical and behavior changes so you can properly determine if they are using spice. By simply recognizing these things you can make a conscious decision whether you need to look a little further.

Slang Terms used to describe Spice:

- K2
- Yucatan Fire
- Fake weed
- Bombay blue
- Bliss
- JWH- 250
- Fake marijuana
- Skunk
- Herbal incense
- Genie
- JWH- 018
- K3
- Blaze
- Moon rocks
- Black mamba
- Zohai
- JWH- 073
- Nice

Slang Terms used to describe how they feel:

- Faded
- Stoned
- Blunted
- Blitzed
- Wrecked
- Baked
- Loaded
- Blazed
- Lit
- Smoked out
- High
- Blown
- Gone
- Toked

Paraphernalia to look for:

Rolling papers

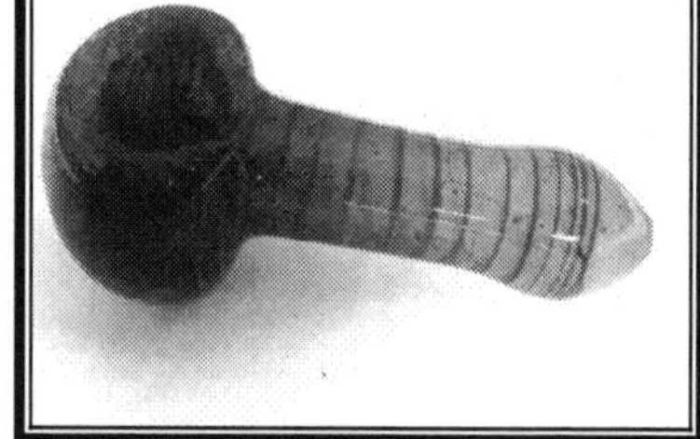

Glass pipe

Glass bong

Eye drops

Silver bags in trash can

Lighters with burn marks on the bottom

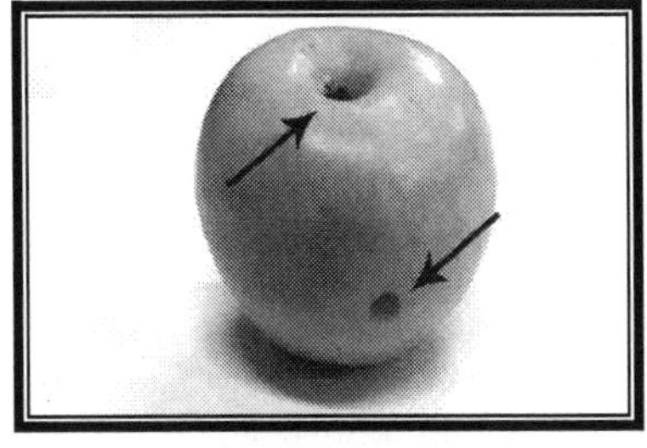

Apple with hole on top and the side

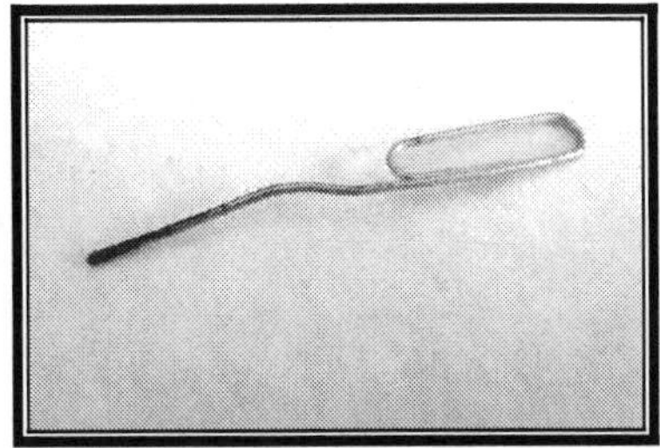

Straightened paper clip

Roaches in ashtray or trash can

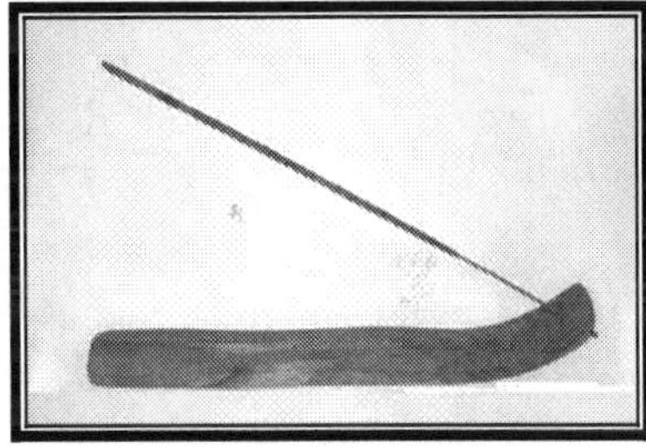

Incense

Deodorizer

Cigar tobacco in trash can

Cigars "Cigarillos"

Physical changes:

When it comes to your teens physical appearance, there are a few obvious signs to look out for. Your teen may appear agitated and have uncontrolled convulsive body movement. You may also notice your teen appears to have a pale complexion and is sweating profusely.

I took spice one time and let me tell you, I can't believe this stuff is legal! I was at a friend's house and he told me it was just like marijuana. Well it wasn't. I can remember that it seemed like everything in the room was in slow motion. I felt like someone was pushing down on my shoulders. We could not stop laughing even when there wasn't anything funny. All we could do was sit there on the couch slumped over and not move. We only had a little bit so I couldn't imagine what a teen would experience with a large amount.

Some teens have reported having seizures, a lack in pain response, and even vomiting. Because the chemical components used in spice are not always the same, the physical changes can vary slightly. You can go on the internet and search spice drug videos and see teens take the drug and what the effects were. Teens video tape everything especially since most teens have smart phones with cameras.

Behavior changes:

Teens may experience severe paranoia or delusions as spice is considered a hallucinogen. The most common paranoia and delusions I have heard are that they believe people are watching or following them, people are outside the window or in bushes, and everyone is conspiring against them. This behavior can intensify based on their current state of mind. If they use spice when they are sad or depressed, paranoia can be very intense. If they use spice when they are happy or content, then they may experience little to no paranoia.

> Hallucinations are quite a common behavior change. They may think that everything is moving in slow motion, have uncontrollable laughter when nothing is funny, or even think that people around them are doing things that they aren't really doing. They may appear very relaxed or unresponsive at the same time because they are caught in their hallucinations.

It's pretty scary when you think about it. Spice is totally legal in most states with very real side effects. When teens are under the impression that something is legal and will also change their state of mind, they are even more likely to try it. We were all a teen once so you should know where I am coming from. Teens don't think about the bad side effects of something, they only care about how good it can make them feel. Teens have died from using spice but that certainly doesn't stop them from trying it.

The amount of teens using spice is increasing every year. Being most common amongst high school students this should be a real cause for concern. When you hear about drug abuse they don't tell you about the legal drugs that are also being abused. Those are the drugs that you need to be more concerned about than anything else and that's because they are the drugs that your teen will have the easiest access to.

You need to look beyond the obvious signs and stay in tune with your teen. Who they choose to surround themselves with, what you notice lying around their room no matter how small it may appear, along with your teens physical and/or behavior changes will all play a key role in knowing if your teen is hiding something from you. Don't be paranoid, just be aware!

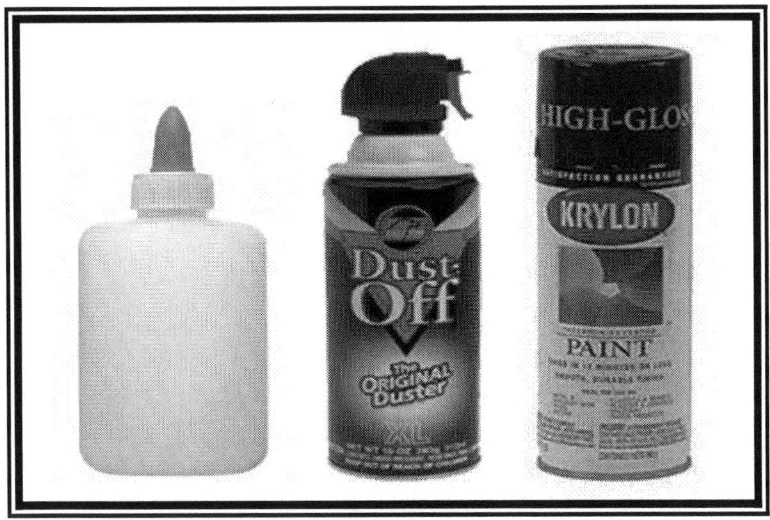

INHALANTS

in ◦ ha ◦ lant

a substance in the form of a vapor of gas that is inhaled, abused for its intoxicating effect

"The use of inhalants is a big concern since these products are legal and can result in irreparable brain damage or death"

– Charles Curie

INHALANTS

Studies show that the primary abusers of inhalants are adolescents ages 12 to 17; in 2008, 1.1 percent using inhalants in the past month. Of the 729,000 people aged 12 and older who tried inhalants for the first time within the previous year, approximately 67 percent were under the age of 18 when they first used.

"National Survey on Drug Use and Health"

Inhalants are considered to be your common every day household products that are abused by inhaling the fumes or vapors. The effects are similar to alcohol intoxication or marijuana but far more dangerous. Teens may pour the inhalant on a rag and sniff it, spray the inside of a bag to inhale the fumes, or directly sniff the container. Vegetable cooking spray, helium, keyboard duster, glue, paint and paint thinners, whipped cream cans, and felt tip markers are among the most commonly used by teens. Sure, most people have inhaled helium at some time because they like how it changes their voice. That's not a crime, but when you abuse the inhalant or you are using a product not for its intended purpose then you could have a problem.

I would say inhalants are very common among early teens because they are so easily accessible. You can go buy most inhalants at any convenience or hardware store for only a few dollars. Inhaling these fumes in large doses can cause brain and throat damage and even death. Inhalants can cause your teen to not function properly, lose complete track of time or even drop out of school. Basically, if you notice a bunch of keyboard dusters, glue bottles, or aerosol cans laying around their room your teen may be using those products as an inhalant and not for its actual intended purpose.

It's important to pay attention to your teens slang when talking to their friends, things your teen may leave lying around their room or in their trash can, physical and behavior changes so you can properly determine if they are using inhalants. By simply recognizing these things you can make a conscious decision whether you need to look a little further.

Slang Terms used to describe Inhalants:

- Huff
- Duster
- Air blast
- Purple haze
- Whiteout
- Kick
- Whippets
- Snappers
- Gas
- Bolt
- Locker room
- Bang
- Poppers
- Bullet bolt
- Quicksilver
- Climax
- Moon gas
- Satan's secret
- Medusa
- Nitrous
- Honey oil
- Liquid incense
- Laughing gas
- Rush
- Highball
- Snotballs
- Buzz bomb
- Poor man's pot
- Toilet water
- Hippie crack
- Blue bottle
- Oz

Slang Terms used to describe how they feel:

- Bagging
- Get dusted
- Huffing
- Blasted
- Gassed up
- Glading

 **Paraphernalia to look for:**

Keyboard duster

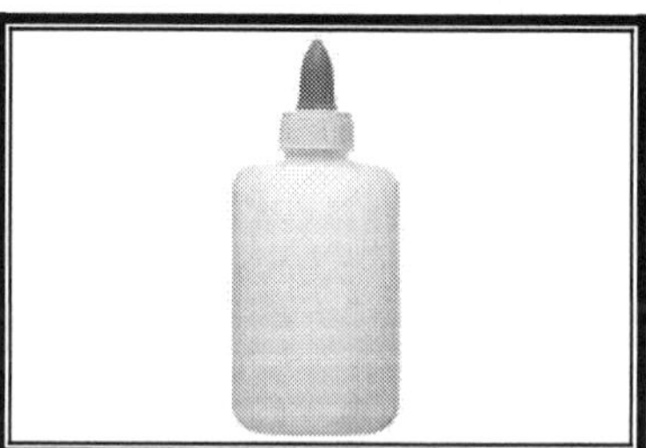

Glue

Room deodorizer

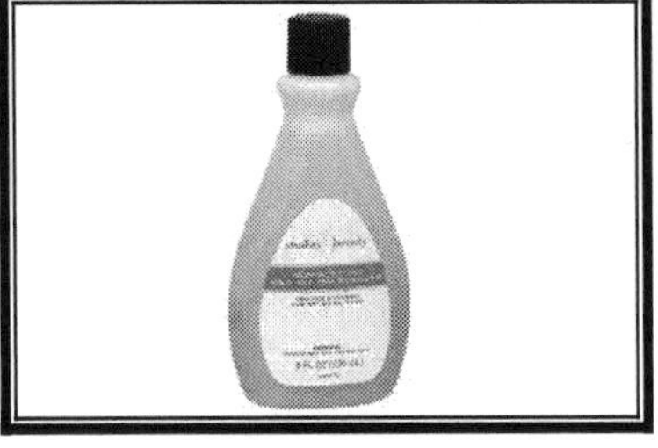

Nail polish remover

Butane lighter fluid

Paint thinner

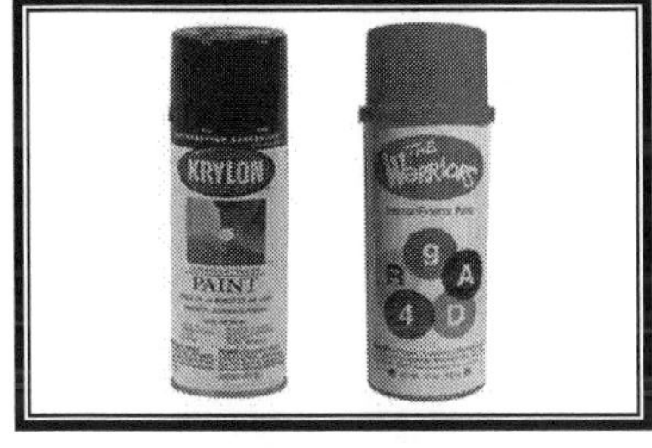

Spray paint

Vegetable cooking spray

Gasoline

Portable propane tanks

Hairspray

Whiteout

Aerosol canisters

Scotch gard

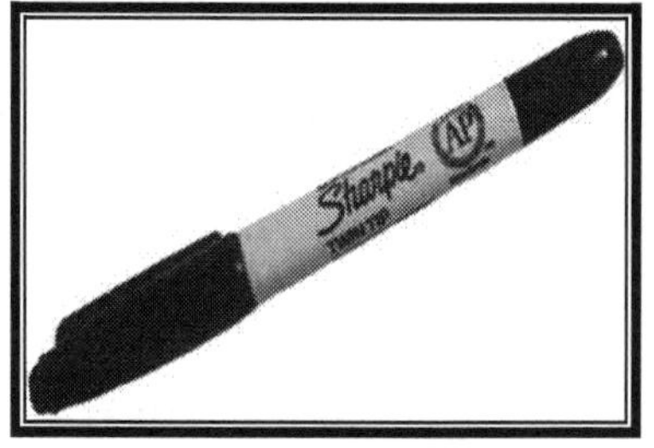

Felt tip markers

Whipped cream cans

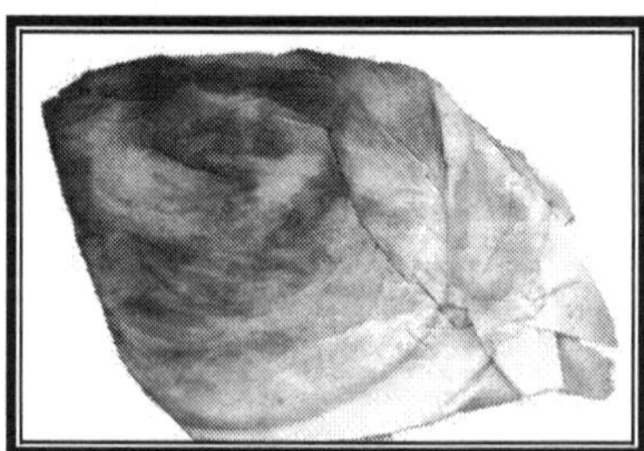

Chemical soaked rags

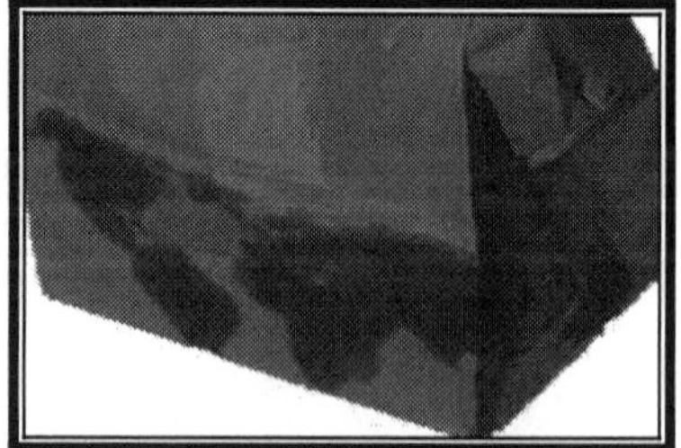

Paper bags with dark stain in trash cans

 **Physical changes:**

When it comes to your teens physical appearance, there are a few obvious signs to look out for. Since inhalant types vary so do the physical changes. The main physical change they all have in common are that it slows them down. Rather than a pick me up drug, it slows their movement, their brain activity, and speech patterns.

If your teen is using an inhalant you will definitely notice a chemical smell on their breath. Since they inhale by breathing in chemicals through their mouth, the smell will remain on their breath for a little while after. The taste buds are also affected by this so they will eat less and lose weight as a result. They will also have extreme face thinning.

Inhalants will also cause breathing problems. They may have wheezing, extreme coughing and other breathing difficulties on more of a constant basis. You can't breathe in toxic chemicals and not have it affect your breathing patterns. Dilated pupils, blood shot eyes, and staggered walking are also physical changes you should pay attention to.

 **Behavior changes:**

Your teen will seem extremely withdrawn from family and spend a lot of time in their room or with friends. Teens can go through several cans of inhalants within a few days so they tend to get stuck in their own little world. They will have increased mood swings and appear very agitated.

I used to know a few people in junior high school who would sniff glue. They would talk about how it made them light headed and how they could not concentrate in classes. The constant use of inhalants will cause a loss in concentration, inability to function in class, failing grades, missing classes or even dropping out of school altogether. It's almost like inhalants make teens appear very out of it or in la la land.

A teens room becomes very messy. You may notice several of the same empty aerosol cans laying around their room or in their trash can. If you do, then there is a cause for concern. You don't go through five cans of keyboard duster or eight bottles of glue as a teen.

You see, inhalants are the type of drug that your teen may be likely to leave laying around their room. They are your common every day household products so they wouldn't seem out of place, but it is the amount of empty household items you see laying around in their room that you need to pay attention to. Teens abuse inhalants because it makes them feel light headed, they are easy to get ahold of, and their friends are doing it. Inhalants are usually not used on their own but more so among friends. Once they develop a habit then they will start to use the inhalant by themselves.

A total addiction to inhalants isn't very common but that doesn't mean that they aren't being abused. It's usually a short addiction and then they grow out of it. For instance, I had friends who sniffed glue in high school and then graduated and never touched it again. Does that mean that you just should do nothing because they will eventually grow out of it? Absolutely not. Abusing a inhalant can cause severe long term brain damage. After all, there is a warning label on all inhalants. Flammable and not for human consumption are pretty good indicators that they can cause health problems if inhaled.

You need to look beyond the obvious signs and stay in tune with your teen. Who they choose to surround themselves with, what you notice lying around their room no matter how small it may appear, along with your teens physical and/or behavior changes will all play a key role in knowing if your teen is hiding something from you. Don't be paranoid, just be aware!

NOW WHAT?

Don't panic! Don't freak out! Take a deep breath and let's try to first understand why your teen is abusing drugs. Most teens abuse because they are bored. Think about it, when your teen is bored they hang out with their friends more often, attend more parties, or spend a lot of time in their room. Drugs provide a way for your teen to fit in with their friends and have fun. Although drugs are dangerous, teens don't think about the consequences at the time. They especially don't think that anything bad could happen to them. Drugs are addictive in nature so therefore they become time consuming. If your teen isn't involved in school programs, sports, or some other kind of activity then they are more likely to experiment with drugs. The more free time your teen has the more they will look for other things to do to fill their time.

There is a difference between your teen using drugs for recreational purposes versus on a constant basis. For instance, your teen may use ecstasy at a party but not use it again for another six months. On the other hand, your teen could smoke methamphetamine regularly and have a full blown addiction. Knowing if your teen is a recreational user or a constant abuser will help you know how to properly handle the situation.

Your teens physical appearance and behavior changes will tell you which type of drug user, if any, your teen may be. When you look at your teens physical or behavior change you will notice a difference one day and not notice a difference the next because they are back to their normal self. If you notice their physical appearance seems to be changing for the worse over a long period of time then they are likely to be a constant abuser.

If you find out that your teen is struggling with a drug problem you need to get them some help. Rehabilitation centers work great for getting your teen sober and off drugs but they are only a temporary solution. Most rehabilitation centers are only 60-90 day treatment programs and then your teen comes home. Rehabilitation centers are a great start but not the only solution. They will help your teen get back to their normal self before their addiction. Once they come home you need to also do your part as their parent if you are serious about getting your teen the help that they need.

While your teen is going through a rehabilitation program I really suggest that you also get some help and support for yourself. There are support groups available for parents of teens suffering from drug addiction. They are definitely worth going to so you can get the proper support needed during this tough time. No one understands what you are going through more than other parents dealing with the same challenges. They will help you come up with a positive plan to get your teen back on the right track, help you with establishing new boundaries, give you a shoulder to cry on, and offer helpful advice. These programs will help you understand where your teen is coming from so you can be a little more sympathetic to your teen when they come home and continue with their sobriety.

I've always said, "Rehabs are good for getting you sober but if you cannot learn to stay sober in your personal environment then it is all for nothing." The amount of teens that get out of rehabilitation centers and go right back to using drugs is astounding. I believe the reason for this is because most parents assume that rehabilitation centers are the ultimate solution and they don't realize that they also need to make changes in their household when their teen comes home.

Helping your teen to stay sober when they come home is important. You may want to try switching their schools so they can make new friends. Clearing the phone numbers out of their cell phone will help so they cannot contact their drug dealers or those bad influence friends they have. Monitoring their social media accounts is also recommended. You tell your teen that you must have their login information if they want to continue to have computer privileges. Now listen up parents, you only need that information so you can check their private messages and news feed to make sure they aren't associating with their drug abuser friends. It's important that you don't become obsessed with their social media accounts and nitpick at every little thing. You need to remember, you want the lines of communication to remain open with your teen. If you are obsessing over every little thing they do then they will start to shut down and hide more of their private life from you. That's not what you want.

Teens need to feel supported. I know we always want to be a parent first and that's not a bad thing but sometimes we also need to be their friend. You need to find a balance between the two. It's time to start working on building a solid relationship with your teen. Having good boundaries with your teen is very much needed. Make it interactive. You both set boundaries and respect each other not to cross them and if they are crossed then there is a consequence. Boundaries are needed in any relationship and are the key to its survival.

I would also use positive reinforcements with your teen. Instead of focusing on what your teen does wrong try complimenting your teen on what they are doing right. A little recognition for even the smallest thing goes a long way with teens. The words "thank you" or even "I appreciate it" are not used anymore as much as they should. Your job as their parent is to rebuild their self-esteem which the drug use has destroyed.

I really believe that the most successful way to help your teen stay sober is to keep them active. Trust me! If they finish school, get a job, get in a sport or after school program, get their GED, do some volunteer work, or any other activity they have a much higher chance of staying sober or never abusing drugs to begin with. I have been around countless drug abusers throughout my teenage years and into my adulthood so I can tell you firsthand that I have seen the difference it makes. Teens start to experiment with drugs when they don't feel like they have a sense of purpose. If all they do is go to school and come home every day, that isn't very fulfilling or exciting to your teen. If you don't spend a lot of family time together then they look to their friends for that family support. Turning to their friends to fill a void in their life will typically lead to involvement in drugs. That's what you want to avoid. You want your teen to have healthy relationships with their friends and family. Certainly not toxic relationships.

I strongly believe that addiction is all in the mind. Teens who suffer from drug addiction have a certain mind set. It explains why some teens who use drugs suffer from addiction and others don't. If you can work at changing your teens mind set then they can overcome addiction. Many teens have overcome drug addiction and your teen can to. There are professional Neuro Linguistic Programming (NLP) coaches that can work with your teen on changing their mind set and I highly recommend it. I have seen some amazing results.

Finding out that your teen has been using drugs is not the end of the world. The worst thing you can do is freak out and confront your teen. I know it's hard not to jump into action but when you react out of anger you can make the situation worse rather than better. The last thing you want to do is tell your teen how worthless they are or how awful they are because they are using drugs. The goal is to get them some help to deal with their addiction and anger isn't going to help you reach that goal. Instead, you need to let your teen know that you care about them and want to support them in the decisions that they make. Start by making some changes in your household, get your teen into a rehabilitation program whether it is a live in or outpatient program, start attending a parents support group, and continue to love and support your teen through their drug abuse problems.

Teens make mistakes and any addiction starts with one bad choice they made. We were all a teen at one time and we tend to forget that. At some point we as parents expect our teens to start acting like adults. But at what point do we gradually start to prepare them for that stage in their life cycle? Think about it, we tell our teen to "grow up" but when have you showed them what growing up is all about? Instead they have all the pressures of high school, their family life, their social life, and preparing to go to college or getting a job all at the same time. That is a lot for a teen to deal with so when they go out with their friends to have a good time they could make a bad decision. If drugs are available and they are told how good the drug is going to make them feel, they may decide to try them.

With this guide you are now aware of the slang terms that they use with their friends, what paraphernalia to look for in their room or car, the physical and behavior changes the drug will cause, and the proper steps you need to take to get your teen the help that they need. By knowing all of this you are aware of the warning signs and can help a situation before it leads to an addiction. I wish my parents knew what to look for because maybe I could have been saved many years before I was. Just remember to stay involved in your teens personal and social life and it will tell you everything you need to know.

MY STORY

I was born in Newport Beach California in 1981. I am the oldest child with a brother born 3 years after me. I grew up with both parents living under the same roof in a posh neighborhood in Lake Forest California. Our community was close knit, every night we ate dinner together as a family, my mother was the leader of my girl scout troop, my parents were both hard working, and everyone used to always tell me how lucky I was to have the perfect family.

When I was about 17 my parents were going through a separation. Leading up to their separation there was a lot of arguing between my parents to the point that we as their children could see a divorce coming. My dad was more of the authoritarian and my mom was more of the caretaker if I had to give them a label. Once they got divorced our lives seemingly went forward, however my family dynamics had really changed. My dad stopped coming around even though he lived down the street. My brother was fighting his own battles with being a preteen and he had to go to a private school out of state so he would graduate high school. So it was just me and my mom.

My mom started dating again so she was away from the house every weekend. Plus she worked during the week so she was gone a lot. As a teen I loved it. I thought it was great because I could do what I want, I had the house to myself, and had my independence. It was like a newfound freedom that I never had before. While I had my independence, which to a teenager it is great thing, in reality it wasn't good because I needed structure and that is given by a parent. My mom did everything right as a parent. She provided a roof over my head, food in my mouth, and a close relationship… when she was home.

Looking back, I know that it wasn't the divorce that had an effect on me. It was my parents behavior after the divorce that had the biggest impact. My brother was away at a private school, my dad rarely came around or even called, and my mom was in a new relationship. It was just me! It wasn't my parents fault but when life moves on sometimes parents can forget that their children still need to be given attention.

At the time I just felt that my family was being ripped apart so I started spending a lot more time with my friends. Growing up I was always the responsible friend. Had been working since I was just 14, didn't get into trouble, was a long time girl scout, drugs were around but I had no desire to do them. Young girls would really look up to me.

Well I started spending more time with my friends and less time at home. Not because I didn't want to be home but because no one was home for me to spend time with. So naturally I navigated towards hanging out with my friends day and night. Within six months I dropped out of high school just two classes away from graduating and quit my job. It started with attending parties on the weekends and drinking alcohol. Alcohol was at every party I ever went to once I turned 16. And when teens drink alcohol they drink to get drunk. Social drinking doesn't exist at that age. Then it moved to drinking and smoking marijuana on occasion. I moved out of my mom's house and in with my friends so we can spend more time together. I really acted like I had absolutely no responsibilities. My friends and I would drink and smoke marijuana every day, go shopping with stolen money and fake checks, stay in hotel rooms for weeks at a time, and just party. Never stopped to think about my future, my responsibilities, my consequences, or anything else. Every day was a party when I was 17. This was just our life.

By the time I was 18 I was living in my car with two friends. Not because I needed to be homeless but because my friends were homeless and I didn't want them to be alone. I met a guy that I really liked and started to hang out with him all the time. I can remember him buying me cigarettes and soda and thinking that this was a good man because I have never had a guy buy me anything before. He was 25 at the time so much older than I was. It turned out that he was a methamphetamine dealer. He started to give the drug to my friends and they would all do it while we sat in my car. At first I passed and didn't try it. It wasn't long, maybe only a few days later, that I also began snorting methamphetamine just like my friends. My life at that point had taken a major turn.

I ended up getting an apartment with my drug dealer boyfriend and needed to come up with a way to pay for our bills and drugs. We were using methamphetamine all day every day. We would smoke and snort methamphetamine all day long for three or four days then sleep for an entire day. Wake up and repeat the same cycle all over again. Stealing was the only way I knew how to get money quickly because I had gotten away with it when I was with my friends before. I stole $80,000 from my relatives and spent it all on drugs and nonsense. All that money just spent on nothing. I never thought about the fact that I could get arrested for stealing or that I was doing anything wrong. Well I was dead wrong. I was arrested for stealing the $80,000 and spent thirty days in the county jail. I got out of jail and went back to my same relationship and same situation. My relationship was physically abusive but I had hit rock bottom that I didn't care anymore. I can remember calling my family to say goodbye because I didn't want to live anymore.

My life had been turned upside down and I really didn't see a way out. My mom and I talked every day and she was always my rock through everything. But the drugs had such a hold on me that I didn't realize I always had a way out. I could have gone home at any time but I was so "in love" with my boyfriend I stayed in my situation because I loved the drugs. By the time I was 22 years old I was in more trouble. I stole another $250,000 while I was on drugs and was sentenced to 16 months in state prison. After my mom pleaded with the District Attorney to let me stay close to home, I was allowed to spend my sentence in a local county jail. I spent a total of 8 months in the county jail. I didn't realize it at the time but that was me being saved.

The fact is, when I spent some time in jail I realized that the only people there to support me was my family. My mom had a full time job but came to visit me every day she was allowed, wrote to me every week, put money on my books so I could have snacks to eat, and accepted my collect calls daily. She never told me how I was a failure, or how I really screwed up. Instead, she showed me how much she loved me and was there to help me when no one else was.

The drugs had me doing things that I would have never done if I wasn't high. I was stealing from my own family just to feed my addiction, I never thought about any consequences, I stayed in an abusive relationship, and I even went to jail a few times. The experiences that I had while on drugs is an experience I hope no teen ever goes through. I went through so much more than I can cover in just a few pages.

Today, I have been clean and sober over nine years. I choose not to focus on my sobriety date and just embrace what life has to offer me now. I don't regret my past experiences because they have formed me into the strong woman that I am today. If I never struggled through addiction then I wouldn't be here to help families of teens today who are struggling with the same issues. I could have never done it without the support of my family. My mother and brother are my best friends and we are closer than ever now. My dad and I have certainly mended our relationship and he is very active in my life and the life of my child.

My biggest "ah ha" moment when I reflect back on my teen years is that not only do my actions affect myself, but they affect everyone around me. My entire family was impacted in major ways by my mistakes and I never took the time to consider that. When I was a teen I only thought about myself. My parents gave up everything that they had worked so hard for to try and help me gain my life back. I am so grateful and blessed to have the family that I have. I want nothing more than my parents to be proud of the woman that I have become despite my past struggles.

My hope is that if you do find that your teen is using drugs that you don't turn your back on them, tell them how horrible they are, or just think that there is no hope. There is always hope! It's a time for you to come together as a family, not be torn apart. Just remember that every teen has their own problems and they all handle situations differently. Sometimes you need to take a step back and view life from your teens perspective and you may see where the break is that is causing your teen to want to use drugs. I hope you find this guide helpful. I want every parent to be aware of the warning signs of teen drug abuse so they can stop any addiction before it even starts.

INDEX

C

D

T

U

V

Did you find this reference guide helpful?

I would love to hear from you if *Slipping Away* has had an impact on your life or the life of someone you know.

Send your letters to:

Email: info@slippingawaybook.com

Fax: (888) 941-9257

Website: www.SlippingAwayBook.com and www.JenniferKobuki.com

Made in the USA
Columbia, SC
14 March 2022

57678697R00065